THE PERIODIC TABLE

ELEMENTS WITH STYLE!

KINGFISHER
NEW YORK

THE PERIODIC TABLE

ELEMENTS WITH STYLE!

| 1 H — HYDROGEN |
3 Li — LITHIUM	4 Be — BERYLLIUM
11 Na — SODIUM	12 Mg — MAGNESIUM
19 K — POTASSIUM	20 Ca — CALCIUM
37 Rb — RUBIDIUM	38 Sr — STRONTIUM
55 Cs — CESIUM	56 Ba — BARIUM
87 Fr — FRANCIUM	88 Ra — RADIUM

21 Sc SCANDIUM	22 Ti TITANIUM	23 V VANADIUM	24 Cr CHROMIUM	25 Mn MANGANESE	26 Fe IRON	27 Co COBALT	28 Ni NICKEL	29 Cu COPPER
39 Y YTTRIUM	40 Zr ZIRCONIUM	41 Nb NIOBIUM	42 Mo MOLYBDENUM	43 Tc TECHNETIUM	44 Ru RUTHENIUM	45 Rh RHODIUM	46 Pd PALLADIUM	47 Ag SILVER
71 Lu LUTETIUM	72 Hf HAFNIUM	73 Ta TANTALUM	74 W TUNGSTEN	75 Re RHENIUM	76 Os OSMIUM	77 Ir IRIDIUM	78 Pt PLATINUM	79 Au GOLD
103 Lr LAWRENCIUM	104 Rf RUTHERFORDIUM	105 Db DUBNIUM	106 Sg SEABORGIUM	107 Bh BOHRIUM	108 Hs HASSIUM	109 Mt MEITNERIUM	110 Ds DARMSTADTIUM	111 Rg ROENTGENIUM

| 57 La LANTHANUM | 58 Ce CERIUM | 59 Pr PRASEODYMIUM | 60 Nd NEODYMIUM | 61 Pm PROMETHIUM | 62 Sm SAMARIUM | 63 Eu EUROPIUM | 64 Gd GADOLINIUM | 65 Tb TERBIUM |
| 89 Ac ACTINIUM | 90 Th THORIUM | 91 Pa PROTACTINIUM | 92 U URANIUM | 93 Np NEPTUNIUM | 94 Pu PLUTONIUM | 95 Am AMERICIUM | 96 Cm CURIUM | 97 Bk BERKELIUM |

KINGFISHER
NEW YORK

KINGFISHER
LONDON & NEW YORK

Text and design copyright © Toucan Books Ltd. 2007
Based on an original concept by Toucan Books Ltd.
Illustrations copyright © Simon Basher 2007

First published 2007 by Kingfisher
This expanded and updated edition published 2015

Published in the United States by Kingfisher,
175 Fifth Ave., New York, NY 10010
Kingfisher is an imprint of Macmillan Children's Books, London.
All rights reserved.

Science Consultant: Dr. Christopher Hutchinson
Consultant: Dr. Mark Winter
Dr. Winter is a senior lecturer of chemistry at the University of Sheffield,
England, and the author of www.webelements.com.
This book uses data adapted from www.webelements.com.

Designed and created by Basher, www.basherbooks.com
Text written by Adrian Dingle and Dan Green

Dedicated to Ella Marbrook

Distributed in the U.S. and Canada by Macmillan, 175 Fifth Ave.,
New York, NY 10010

Library of Congress Cataloging-in-Publication data has been applied for.

ISBN: 978-0-7534-7196-8 (HC)
ISBN: 978-0-7534-7197-5 (PB)

Kingfisher books are available for special promotions and premiums.
For details contact: Special Markets Department, Macmillan,
175 Fifth Ave., New York, NY 10010.

For more information about Kingfisher books, please visit
www.kingfisherbooks.com

Printed in China
9 8 7 6 5 4 3 2
2TR/0116/WKT/UG/128MA

CONTENTS

The Periodic Table
Introduction

Everything in the world is made of elements—substances that cannot be broken down or made into anything simpler by chemical reactions. Each element has its own unique personality. Many, such as gold, silver, and lead, have been known for millenia. Others, such as livermorium, have been created in high-tech labs, only as recently as 2000, and chemists are busy making more.

The periodic table was the brainchild of Siberian superchemist Dmitri Mendeleev. In 1869, he arranged the known elements into groups (columns) and periods (rows), leaving gaps in his table for chemical elements that were still undiscovered at the time. Today the gaps have been filled, and there are a total of 118 known elements, but there may be others that are yet undiscovered. The vertical groups of the table make up "families"—all closely related and liking the same sorts of chemical shenanigans. In this book you'll meet every one of 118 characters, from the lightest to the heaviest, and including all the breakaways and mavericks that like to do things their own way. . .

Mendelevium (named after Mendeleev)

1 Hydrogen

- ✳ Symbol: H
- ✳ Atomic number: 1
- ✳ Atomic weight: 1.008
- ✳ Color: None
- ✳ Standard state: Gas at 25°C (77°F)
- ✳ Classification: Nonmetallic

I may be undersized, but don't underestimate me. I'm a petite package who packs a punch, and I have a fiery character to boot—always remember that I'm *numero uno*! I am the simplest and lightest of all the elements, the most abundant in the Universe, and the source of everything in it—from matter and energy to life. I'm what powers nuclear fusion in the stars, and I'm the building block for all of the other elements of the periodic table.

On Earth, I exist as a gas consisting of a pair of hydrogen atoms (H_2). Things always happen with a bang when I'm around. I'm extraordinarily flammable. I was once used to fill airships, until a few fatal explosions ended my career. In the future, I am set to become important in fuel cells—a clean and efficient way of generating electricity.

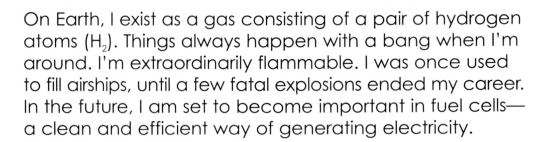

Date of discovery: 1766

- ● Density   0.082 g/l
- ● Melting point   −259.14°C (−434.45°F)
- ● Boiling point   −252.87°C (−423.17°F)

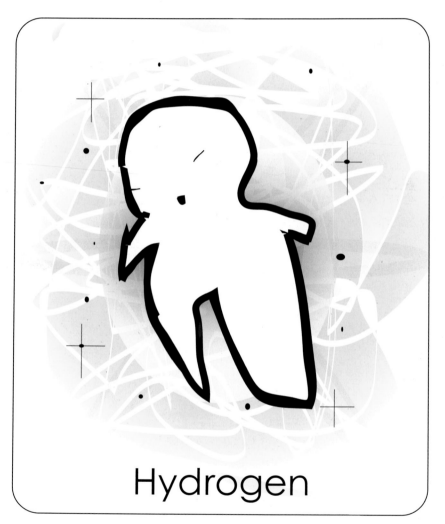

Hydrogen

CHAPTER 1

The Alkali Metals

A rowdy bunch of rebels, these elements have a reputation for extremely reactive behavior. Chemically too feisty to be found unchanged in nature, this group is closer and more alike than any other group of the periodic table. All members are low-density, soft metals. When added to water, they turn it alkaline. Their dangerous desperation to lose their outer electron increases with their atomic number, and as soon as they come into contact with almost anything (including air), a violently explosive reaction follows. . .

3

Li

LITHIUM

11

Na

SODIUM

19

K

POTASSIUM

37

Rb

RUBIDIUM

55

Cs

CESIUM

87

Fr

FRANCIUM

3 Lithium

■ The Alkali Metals

- ✴ Symbol: Li
- ✴ Atomic number: 3
- ✴ Atomic weight: 6.941

- ✴ Color: Silvery gray/white
- ✴ Standard state: Solid at 25°C (77°F)
- ✴ Classification: Metallic

The lightest of all metals on the periodic table and the first, I am a real soft touch. You can easily slice me with a knife, but when I'm combined with other metals like aluminum, I make very strong (and light) alloys. These qualities make me popular with the aerospace industry.

I am generally a useful and very helpful character. You can find me acting as the positive half of many batteries and as part of high-performance, industrial lubricants.

As lithium chloride (me plus chlorine), I'm remarkably good at absorbing large amounts of water. Taken as lithium carbonate (me, oxygen, and carbon), I help restore damaged personalities—calming and relieving sufferers of mental illnesses such as bipolar disorder.

Date of discovery: 1817

- ● Density   0.535 g/cm³
- ● Melting point 180.54°C (356.97°F)
- ● Boiling point   1,342°C (2,448°F)

Lithium

11 Sodium

■ The Alkali Metals

✴ Symbol: Na
✴ Atomic number: 11
✴ Atomic weight: 22.990

✴ Color: Gray/white
✴ Standard state: Solid at 25°C (77°F)
✴ Classification: Metallic

I'm a complete live wire—high-strung and volatile—
but I get along well with everyone and make strong,
long-lasting friendships. I'm a gray-colored metal that's
soft enough to be cut with a knife. I'm really reactive—
you need to store me under oil to stop me from chemically
reacting with the oxygen in air, and I'll explode into flames
on contact with water!

I form lots of common compounds, like sodium chloride
(salt) and sodium carbonate (dishwashing soap), which
are all solid and very stable owing to their strong bonds.
My ions (negative particles) are very soluble and are the
reason why the sea is salty. I give streetlights their orange
glow, and I am used in nuclear reactors as a coolant
because I conduct heat really well.

Date of discovery: 1807

● Density   0.968 g/cm³
● Melting point 97.72°C (207.9°F)
● Boiling point   883°C (1,621°F)

Sodium

19 **Potassium**

■ The Alkali Metals

* Symbol: K
* Atomic number: 19
* Atomic weight: 39.098

* Color: Silver
* Standard state: Solid at 25°C (77°F)
* Classification: Metallic

I am sodium's twin. I am soft and react with air, so storing me under oil is essential. This small precaution keeps me isolated from contact with air or water. My ions can be easily detected in any substance since they give off a bright lilac flame. Just as dazzling is my explosive reaction with water, which is even stronger than that of sodium.

Everyone knows that I can be found in bananas, but I bet you didn't know that I am central to many processes in your body. Most vitally, I aid the function of the nerves, allowing the brain to transmit information to the muscles. But too much of me in the body can lead to a heart attack, and this is my darker side—in the U.S., potassium chloride is used in the lethal injections that kill Death Row prisoners.

Date of discovery: 1807

● Density   0.856 g/cm³
● Melting point 63.38°C (146.08°F)
● Boiling point 759°C (1,398°F)

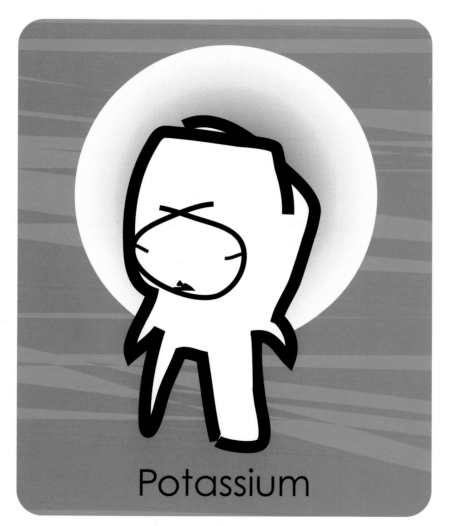

Potassium

37 Rubidium

■ The Alkali Metals

* Symbol: Rb
* Atomic number: 37
* Atomic weight: 85.468
* Color: Silvery
* Standard state: Solid at 25°C (77°F)
* Classification: Metallic

Another big softy in a group of squishy metals, I'm barely solid at room temperature. I'm a shy and elusive type and like to pretend to be one of the other Group 1 elements. In fact, I can disguise myself so well, it can be hard to tell us apart. Like the rest of the gang, I'm superreactive. I go off with a very big bang on contact with air or water.

I'm scarce and hard to find, but even so, I'm the element of choice when it comes to low-power lasers. Printers, telecoms networks using fiber-optic cable, and store barcode readers all use me in their diode laser systems. (Lasers take on a characteristic red-pink color.) I'm also used in compact, superaccurate atomic clocks. My tricksy rarity makes me very expensive. Keep your eyes peeled for me in medicines of the future. . .

Date of discovery: 1861

● Density 1.532 g/cm³
● Melting point 39.31°C (102.76°F)
● Boiling point 688°C (1,270°F)

Rubidium

55 Cesium

■ The Alkali Metals

- ✳ Symbol: Cs
- ✳ Atomic number: 55
- ✳ Atomic weight: 132.91
- ✳ Color: Golden tinge
- ✳ Standard state: Solid at 25°C (77°F)
- ✳ Classification: Metallic

Soft and golden, I'm way more exciting than gold. When provoked, I give off a sky-blue light. Of my Group 1 gang, I have the fiercest reaction to water. I keep the beat in atomic clocks— accurate to one second every several hundred thousand years! My nasty radioactive isotope, cesium-137, was a major pollutant after the 1986 Chernobyl nuclear disaster in the former U.S.S.R.

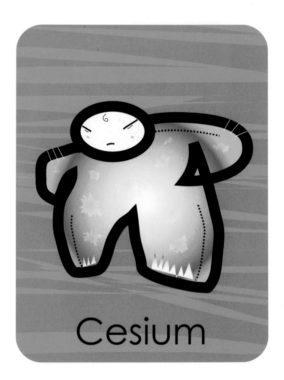

Cesium

Date of discovery: 1860

Cs:
- ● Density — 1.879 g/cm³
- ● Melting point — 28.44°C (83.19°F)
- ● Boiling point — 671°C (1,240°F)

Francium 87
The Alkali Metals ■

* Symbol: Fr
* Atomic number: 87
* Atomic weight: 223.02

* Color: Unknown
* Standard state: Solid at 25°C (77°F)
* Classification: Metallic

Francium

I'm an unstable little critter and I'm very radioactive. With a half-life of only 22 minutes, I don't hang around for long. This makes me extremely rare—no weighable sample has ever existed. That's why my color remains something of a mystery. I'm named after the country; my discoverer, Marguerite Perey, was the first woman to be admitted to the French Academy of Sciences.

Date of discovery: 1939

● Density   2.91 g/cm³
● Melting point 30°C (86°F)
● Boiling point 598°C (1,108°F)

Fr

21

CHAPTER 2
The Alkaline Earth Metals

The "alkaline earths" were once thought to be totally harmless and boring, because they were always found tightly bonded to oxygen. However, once released from these stable compounds, they began to act in the same unruly fashion as their next-door neighbors, the Group 1 family. Another gang of soft metals, these guys react easily and burn fiercely, getting meaner toward the base of the group. All are eager to lose their outer electrons, but this happens less easily than it does for the alkali metals, so they are a little less active.

4

Be

BERYLLIUM

12

Mg

MAGNESIUM

20

Ca

CALCIUM

38

Sr

STRONTIUM

56

Ba

BARIUM

88

Ra

RADIUM

4 Beryllium

■ The Alkaline Earth Metals

✷ Symbol: Be
✷ Atomic number: 4
✷ Atomic weight: 9.0122

✷ Color: Silvery
✷ Standard state: Solid at 25°C (77°F)
✷ Classification: Metallic

Lucky for you, I am shy and secretive and don't get out much. A small amount of me in your body can give you berylliosis, a disease that inflames the lungs and is linked to lung cancer. As a metal, I am soft and silvery, and I'm used mostly in metal alloys, in league with other metals. I make an excellent electrical conductor, and I'm very flexible, too. Because I am so superlight, I also get used in the manufacture of airplanes.

I'm often dug out of the ground as silicates—compounds that I form with silicon and other elements—the most beautiful of which is an emerald. My proudest moment came in 1932 when James Chadwick bombarded me with alpha particles and discovered the neutron. The neutrons that I produce now play a leading role in nuclear chemistry.

Date of discovery: 1797

● Density   1.848 g/cm³
● Melting point   1,287°C (2,349°F)
● Boiling point   2,469°C (4,476°F)

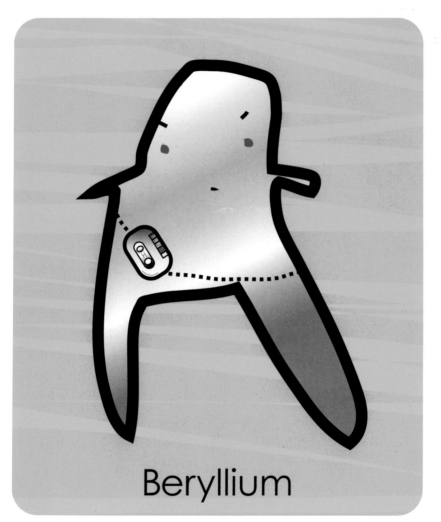

Beryllium

12 **Magnesium**

■ The Alkaline Earth Metals

✴ Symbol: Mg
✴ Atomic number: 12
✴ Atomic weight: 24.305

✴ Color: Silver-white
✴ Standard state: Solid at 25°C (77°F)
✴ Classification: Metallic

I'm happy to mix in any social gathering of the elements, making friends with anyone, even moody hydrogen. I'm sparky, and I always cause a reaction!

I'm a smart aleck, too—I can speed up your body processes and make you rush to the bathroom! The laxatives Epsom salts and milk of magnesia are both made using my salts, which also give a bitter taste to food and can leave a bad taste in your mouth.

I am a silver-white metal and burn with incredible intensity and a bright white light. My splendiferous powers of combustion are used in flashbulbs, distress flares, fireworks, and incendiary bombs. Strong and light, I help make bike frames, car parts, and aircraft engines.

Date of discovery: 1755

● Density   1.738 g/cm³
● Melting point   650°C (1,202°F)
● Boiling point   1,090°C (1,994°F)

Magnesium

20 Calcium

■ The Alkaline Earth Metals

☀ Symbol: Ca
☀ Atomic number: 20
☀ Atomic weight: 40.078

☀ Color: Silvery
☀ Standard state: Solid at 25°C (77°F)
☀ Classification: Metallic

They call me "The Scaffolder" because I make up a large portion of the parts that hold you together— your skeleton and teeth. I'm needed in large amounts as you grow, to build the calcium phosphate of your bones, and as you get older to keep your frame strong.

A reactive metal, I'm soft and silvery in appearance, but I'm a bit harder on the inside. When my ions dissolve in water, it becomes "hard"—detergents won't lather, soap forms a surface scum, and limescale develops on faucets.

I've been known for hundreds of years and am found in common compounds such as lime, cement, chalk, and limestone. All of these are white, have been used in construction, and also have the ability to neutralize acid.

Date of discovery: 1808

● Density   1.550 g/cm³
● Melting point 842°C (1,548°F)
● Boiling point   1,484°C (2,703°F)

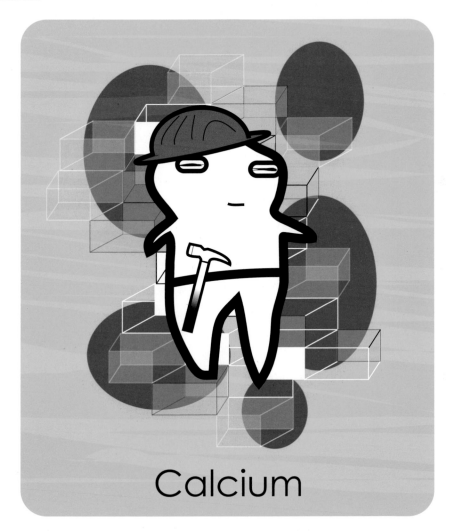

Calcium

38 Strontium

■ The Alkaline Earth Metals

✸ Symbol: Sr
✸ Atomic number: 38
✸ Atomic weight: 87.62

✸ Color: Silvery
✸ Standard state: Solid at 25°C (77°F)
✸ Classification: Metallic

I'm Scottish, named after the town of Strontian where I was discovered. You may see me as a shy, run-of-the-mill, silver-colored metal, but I've got a few surprises up my sleeve. I'll catch your eye with the stunning crimson colors that I give to fireworks. Today my main use is as an additive in the glass of TV sets and computer monitors.

My sneaky radioactive isotope, strontium-90, has the eerie ability to mimic calcium and get absorbed inside growing bones. It releases harmful beta-particle radiation, which causes cancer. In the mid-1900s, nuclear-bomb testing meant that there was a lot of me around. I began to build up in the bodies of children. Luckily, the testing was stopped when scientists realized the potentially horrible consequences.

Date of discovery: 1790

● Density   2.630 g/cm³
● Melting point 777°C (1,431°F)
● Boiling point   1,382°C (2,520°F)

Sr

Strontium

31

56 **Barium**

■ The Alkaline Earth Metals

- ❋ Symbol: Ba
- ❋ Atomic number: 56
- ❋ Atomic weight: 137.33
- ❋ Color: Silver-white
- ❋ Standard state: Solid at 25°C (77°F)
- ❋ Classification: Metallic

One of the heavy metals, I'm a real rocker and more reactive than calcium. My carbonate salt is a deadly rat poison, but my sulfate salt is insoluble and totally indigestible. It's used for "barium meals," which are neither tasty nor nutritious, but are ideal for seeing how you are digesting your food. When excited, my ions give off an apple-green color.

Barium

Date of discovery: 1808

Ba :
- ● Density   3.510 g/cm³
- ● Melting point   727°C (1,341°F)
- ● Boiling point   1,870°C (3,398°F)

Radium 88

The Alkaline Earth Metals ■

* Symbol: Ra
* Atomic number: 88
* Atomic weight: 226.03

* Color: Silver-metallic
* Standard state: Solid at 25°C (77°F)
* Classification: Metallic

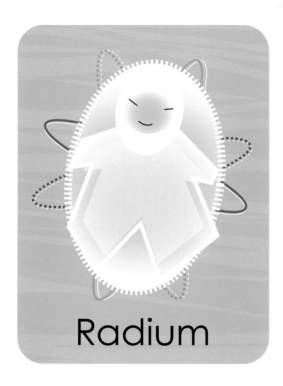

Radium

I am the heaviest of the gang and a completely captivating character. I shine in any social situation. Bright and luminescent (I was used in glow-in-the-dark paint), I am a real stunner. I have the power to ionize air with the radioactive alpha particles that I give off, creating a crackling bright blue aura around me. My name comes from the Latin *radius*, meaning "ray."

Date of discovery: 1898

* Density   5.000 g/cm³
* Melting point   700°C (1,292°F)
* Boiling point   1,737°C (3,159°F)

Ra

CHAPTER 3
The Transition Elements

Groups 3–12

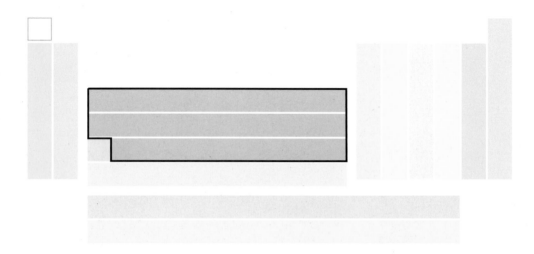

Stuck in the middle of the periodic table, the transition elements are a motley crew of roughnecks. Strapping, robust metals, these guys get involved in literally thousands of industrial applications. Many are catalysts—movers and shakers that kick-start all sorts of important manufacturing reactions. Others use their amazing ability to bond with a wide variety of other elements to form alloys—some of which have changed civilization forever. But it's not all grit and grime: the transition elements love to show up in a dazzling variety of highly colored forms.

21 Sc SCANDIUM

22 Ti TITANIUM

23 V VANADIUM

24 Cr CHROMIUM

25 Mn MANGANESE

26 Fe IRON

27 Co COBALT

28 Ni NICKEL

29 Cu COPPER

30 Zn ZINC

39 Y YTTRIUM

40 Zr ZIRCONIUM

41 Nb NIOBIUM

42 Mo MOLYBDENUM

43 Tc TECHNETIUM

44 Ru RUTHENIUM

45 Rh RHODIUM

46 Pd PALLADIUM

47 Ag SILVER

48 Cd CADMIUM

72 Hf HAFNIUM

73 Ta TANTALUM

74 W TUNGSTEN

75 Re RHENIUM

76 Os OSMIUM

77 Ir IRIDIUM

78 Pt PLATINUM

79 Au GOLD

80 Hg MERCURY

21 Scandium

■ The Transition Elements

- ✳ Symbol: Sc
- ✳ Atomic number: 21
- ✳ Atomic weight: 44.956

- ✳ Color: Silvery-white
- ✳ Standard state: Solid at 25°C (77°F)
- ✳ Classification: Metallic

I'm the very first transition element but don't make a fuss over me. I'm a bit shy. I spend so much time hanging out with the lanthanoids that I'm often included with them in a group called the "rare earth" elements. My name comes from the Latin word for Scandinavia (*Scandia*). I give strength to posh aluminum bike frames and baseball bats.

Scandium

Date of discovery: 1879

 Sc
- ● Density — 2.985 g/cm³
- ● Melting point — 1,541°C (2,806°F)
- ● Boiling point — 2,830°C (5,126°F)

36

Titanium 22

The Transition Elements ▪

- ✳ Symbol: Ti
- ✳ Atomic number: 22
- ✳ Atomic weight: 47.867

- ✳ Color: Clean, gleaming silver
- ✳ Standard state: Solid at 25°C (77°F)
- ✳ Classification: Metallic

Titanium

I am gleaming, extremely hard, and very resistant to any type of chemical attack. As a brilliant-white dioxide compound (me plus two oxygen atoms), I make excellent paint. My main use is for superhard metal alloys whose unrivaled combo of lightness and strength means they often get used in airplane and spacecraft manufacturing.

Date of discovery: 1791

- ● Density   4.507 g/cm³
- ● Melting point 1,668°C (3,034°F)
- ● Boiling point   3,287°C (5,949°F)

Ti

23 Vanadium

■ The Transition Elements

* ✴ Symbol: V
* ✴ Atomic number: 23
* ✴ Atomic weight: 50.942

* ✴ Color: Silver-gray
* ✴ Standard state: Solid at 25°C (77°F)
* ✴ Classification: Metallic

My beauty knows no bounds. I am named after the Scandinavian goddess of beauty and love, Vanadis. Depending on my state (the charge of my various ions), I can make a rainbow of brilliant and beautiful purple, green, blue, and yellow solutions.

Like most transition metals, my colorful compounds can be used as catalysts (substances that allow chemical reactions to occur more freely). I am an essential catalyst in the "contact process" that is used to manufacture sulfuric acid, arguably the most important industrial chemical in the world today. I make up part of a crucial steel alloy that was used in Henry Ford's Model-T cars, so without me, there may never have been an auto industry.

Date of discovery: 1801

● Density   6.110 g/cm³
● Melting point 1,910°C (3,470°F)
● Boiling point 3,407°C (6,165°F)

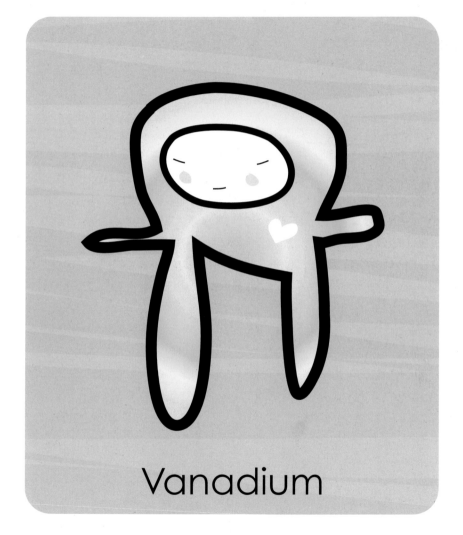

Vanadium

24 Chromium

■ The Transition Elements

- ✸ Symbol: Cr
- ✸ Atomic number: 24
- ✸ Atomic weight: 51.996

- ✸ Color: Supershiny silver
- ✸ Standard state: Solid at 25°C (77°F)
- ✸ Classification: Metallic

I'm totally flash. You may know me as a shiny, decorative metal on bikes and fancy kitchen equipment, but I am much more than just a pretty face. My name comes from the Greek word *chroma*, which means "color," because I can appear in an impressive range of funky shades (different oxidation states)—from red to green, orange, and yellow. I am responsible for the brilliant red color of rubies, and I put the "stainless" into stainless steel. There's no tarnishing my record!

It's easy to take a shine to me—just polish me with a cloth. I'm almost completely resistant to corrosion. Because of this, I was once used as a protective layer (a plating) to stop steel surfaces from rusting. I gave old cars their classic, mirrored-metal look. These days, most cars use plastic.

Date of discovery: 1797

- ● Density   7.140 g/cm³
- ● Melting point 1,907°C (3,465°F)
- ● Boiling point   2,671°C (4,840°F)

Chromium

25 Manganese

■ The Transition Elements

* Symbol: Mn
* Atomic number: 25
* Atomic weight: 54.938

* Color: Silvery
* Standard state: Solid at 25°C (77°F)
* Classification: Metallic

I'm a hard and brittle element. I am found in large amounts in the rocks of the ocean floor, and I'm most widely used in steel manufacturing. Steel is much stronger when it is joined with me in an alloy.

Like many of the other transition metals, I can exist in many different forms (oxidation states), and I change my appearance like an undercover agent—I can be pink, black, green, or dark purple.

Spend too long with me, and I'll mess with your mind. I play an important role in the body, but too much of me can give you "manganese madness," a terrifying psychiatric condition that causes hallucinations. I have also been associated with Parkinson's disease.

Date of discovery: 1774

● Density   7.470 g/cm^3
● Melting point   1,246°C (2,275°F)
● Boiling point   2,061°C (3,742°F)

Manganese

26 **Iron**

The Transition Elements

* Symbol: Fe
* Atomic number: 26
* Atomic weight: 55.845

* Color: Gray
* Standard state: Solid at 25°C (77°F)
* Classification: Metallic

I am at the center of everything. I am the hub. As the main element in your blood's hemoglobin—the substance that transports oxygen throughout the body—I keep you alive. Journey to the center of Earth, and you'll find me there at the core of things. I am the most abundant element in the planet you live on, and I am at the heart of civilization, too.

I am the most important metal ever known to humankind. My use for tools and weapons transformed the ancient world; using me for construction and industrialization made the modern world. I'm most useful when I am mixed with small amounts of carbon to produce steel. But I'm not without flaws—I oxidize easily when exposed to air and water, making rust a constant problem.

Earliest known use: c. 2500 B.C.

● Density   7.874 g/cm³
● Melting point 1,538°C (2,800°F)
● Boiling point   2,861°C (5,182°F)

Iron

27 **Cobalt**

■ The Transition Elements

- ✳ Symbol: Co
- ✳ Atomic number: 27
- ✳ Atomic weight: 58.933
- ✳ Color: Gray
- ✳ Standard state: Solid at 25°C (77°F)
- ✳ Classification: Metallic

Mysterious and attractive, I am the gremlin of the underworld. German miners called me *kobold* ("goblin"). They thought that I stopped them from getting to other more valuable metals, such as silver. For centuries, my compounds have been used to add color to glass. Blue is my best-known shade, but green and pink also feature.

Cobalt

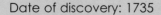

Date of discovery: 1735

Co
- ● Density 8.900 g/cm³
- ● Melting point 1,495°C (2,723°F)
- ● Boiling point 2,927°C (5,301°F)

Nickel 28

The Transition Elements ■

- ☀ Symbol: Ni
- ☀ Atomic number: 28
- ☀ Atomic weight: 58.693

- ☀ Color: Silvery
- ☀ Standard state: Solid at 25°C (77°F)
- ☀ Classification: Metallic

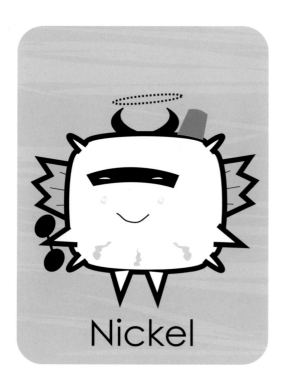

Nickel

I'm a devil in disguise, often mistaken for copper. My name comes from the German word *kupfernickel* ("devil's copper"). I love hanging out with the other transition elements, and I'm great at forming alloys to make materials stronger and more resistant to corrosion. You'll find me charging around batteries and in special heat-resistant materials.

Date of discovery: 1751

- ● Density   8.908 g/cm³
- ● Melting point 1,455°C (2,651°F)
- ● Boiling point   2,913°C (5,275°F)

Ni

29 Copper

The Transition Elements

- Symbol: Cu
- Atomic number: 29
- Atomic weight: 63.546
- Color: Reddish
- Standard state: Solid at 25°C (77°F)
- Classification: Metallic

I am an age-old metal that gave birth to whole chunks of history and launched civilizations. As a pure metal or mixed with tin to make bronze, I have been used for hundreds of years to make ornaments and practical tools. Along with tin, I formed the basis of the Bronze Age.

I am unique among metals in that I have a red hue, but some of my salts are a vivid blue. In fact, many sea creatures have blue blood because of my presence.

I'm the poor relation in a very well-to-do family. Along with silver and gold, we're known as the "coinage metals." However, these days I'm only used in very small amounts in pennies (along with zinc). I am an exceptional conductor of electricity and heat, so I'm also used in wiring.

Earliest known use: c. 4500 B.C.

- Density   8.920 g/cm³
- Melting point   1,084.62°C (1,984.32°F)
- Boiling point   2,927°C (5,301°F)

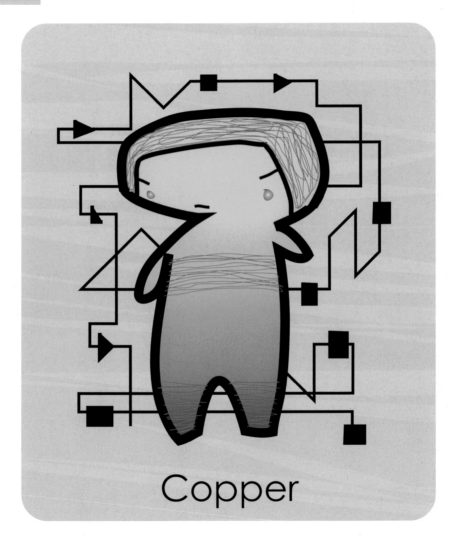

Copper

30 Zinc

■ The Transition Elements

* Symbol: Zn
* Atomic number: 30
* Atomic weight: 65.38

* Color: Bluish-gray
* Standard state: Solid at 25°C (77°F)
* Classification: Metallic

Here to protect and serve, I'm more useful than you'd ever zinc! I'm a very sociable element that's always happy to mix in with other metals. Brass is probably my most well-known alloy, formed when I get together with copper. On my own I can be found in batteries.

With a thin layer of my atoms, I "galvanize" steel, stopping water and oxygen from rusting it away. Even if I am scratched and the steel gets exposed, I quickly form zinc oxide before iron in the steel has a chance to corrode. I also protect people from sunburn as the white zinc oxide sunblock that can be seen on the noses of lifeguards.

What's more, I'm an essential element for lots of body processes, and I can be taken as a dietary supplement.

Date of discovery: 1500

● Density   7.140 g/cm³
● Melting point 419.53°C (787.15°F)
● Boiling point 907°C (1,665°F)

Zinc

39 **Yttrium**

■ The Transition Elements

* ✳ Symbol: Y
* ✳ Atomic number: 39
* ✳ Atomic weight: 88.906
* ✳ Color: Dullish white
* ✳ Standard state: Solid at 25°C (77°F)
* ✳ Classification: Metallic

Rare yet unspectacular as a metal, I make a stunning additive. I spice up all sorts of chemical compounds to make superhard crystals with surprising properties. For example, YAG crystals generate lasers that slice through metal, while YBCO crystals are great superconductors. Like my buddy scandium, I am a "rare earth" element.

Yttrium

Date of discovery: 1794

 Y
- Density   4.472 g/cm³
- Melting point   1,526°C (2,779°F)
- Boiling point   3,336°C (6,037°F)

Zirconium 40
The Transition Elements ■

- ✴ Symbol: Zr
- ✴ Atomic number: 40
- ✴ Atomic weight: 91.224
- ✴ Color: Silvery-white
- ✴ Standard state: Solid at 25°C (77°F)
- ✴ Classification: Metallic

Zirconium

A tough little customer. I'm so heat-resistant that they use me as a ladle for molten metal. I'm impervious to chemical attacks and strong enough to line nuclear reactors. As zirconia, I make gritty little crystals that are as hard as diamond (and just as pretty). Cutting blades made from me are unbelievably sharp. Boy, have I got the edge!

Date of discovery: 1824

- ● Density   6.511 g/cm³
- ● Melting point   1,855°C (3,371°F)
- ● Boiling point   4,409°C (7,968°F)

Zr

53

41 **Niobium**

■ The Transition Elements

* Symbol: Nb
* Atomic number: 41
* Atomic weight: 92.906

* Color: Gray-white
* Standard state: Solid at 25°C (77°F)
* Classification: Metallic

I'm named after the Greek goddess Niobe, daughter of Tantalus, and bear quite a likeness to tantalum. I am a pretty, metal with wild blue, green, yellow, purple, and violet oxides. I like to play it cool and don't easily get involved in chemistry, but you'll see me winking at you occasionally from belly piercings and in superalloys used in rockets.

Niobium

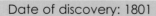

Date of discovery: 1801

Nb
● Density   8.57 g/cm³
● Melting point   2,477°C (4,491°F)
● Boiling point   4,744°C (8,571°F)

Molybdenum 42
The Transition Elements ■

* Symbol: Mo
* Atomic number: 42
* Atomic weight: 95.96

* Color: Gray
* Standard state: Solid at 25°C (77°F)
* Classification: Metallic

Molybdenum

I am your bona fide tough nut, so don't go calling me Molly. When I am added to steel, I make it superresilient and heat-resistant. I am often found mixed up with lead ores, and my name even means "like lead." I am a great friend to growing plants because I help them to capture nitrogen from the atmosphere for their nutrition.

Date of discovery: 1781

● Density   10.280 g/cm³
● Melting point   2,623°C (4,753°F)
● Boiling point   4,639°C (8,382°F)

Mo

43 Technetium

■ The Transition Elements

- ✳ Symbol: Tc
- ✳ Atomic number: 43
- ✳ Atomic weight: 97.907
- ✳ Color: Shiny gray
- ✳ Standard state: Solid at 25°C (77°F)
- ✳ Classification: Metallic

Boo! You wouldn't expect to find a radioactive fellow like me stuck here in the middle of the stable transition elements. But there you go! I'm a nuclear waste product, but a force for the good. My radioactivity allows doctors to look inside bodies and seek out tumors. Tens of thousands of people are injected with me every single day.

Technetium

Date of discovery: 1936

Tc
- ● Density   11.5 g/cm³
- ● Melting point   2,157°C (3,915°F)
- ● Boiling point   4,265°C (7,709°F)

Ruthenium 44

The Transition Elements

- ✴ Symbol: Ru
- ✴ Atomic number: 44
- ✴ Atomic weight: 101.07
- ✴ Color: Silver mirror
- ✴ Standard state: Solid at 25°C (77°F)
- ✴ Classification: Metallic

Ruthenium

I am a secretive element. Not many people have heard of me, and I'd like to keep it that way. I am a member of the flashy platinum group of metals, but I'm not as expensive as some of them. I'm mainly used in electrical circuits, where my superhardness resists general wear and tear. You'll also find me in the nibs of connoisseurs' pens.

Date of discovery: 1844

- ● Density 12.37 g/cm³
- ● Melting point 2,334°C (4,233°F)
- ● Boiling point 4,150°C (7,502°F)

Ru

45 **Rhodium**

■ The Transition Elements

- ✸ Symbol: Rh
- ✸ Atomic number: 45
- ✸ Atomic weight: 102.91
- ✸ Color: Silvery-white
- ✸ Standard state: Solid at 25°C (77°F)
- ✸ Classification: Metallic

I am reassuringly reluctant to react and I'm really rare, which makes me pretty darn expensive. I am untouchable—acids strong enough to dissolve gold won't get anywhere near me. Even so, I'm a dab hand at breaking down molecules. You'll find me with platinum and palladium, tackling greenhouse gases in catalytic converters.

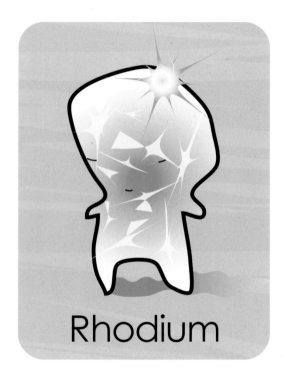

Rhodium

Date of discovery: 1803

Rh:
- ● Density — 12.45 g/cm³
- ● Melting point — 1,964°C (3,567°F)
- ● Boiling point — 3,695°C (6,683°F)

Palladium 46

The Transition Elements ▪

- ✹ Symbol: Pd
- ✹ Atomic number: 46
- ✹ Atomic weight: 106.42

- ✹ Color: Silvery
- ✹ Standard state: Solid at 25°C (77°F)
- ✹ Classification: Metallic

Palladium

I'm a wizard all around the industrial world because of my amazing skill as a catalyzer of reactions. This makes me even more sought after than my close cousin, platinum. The secret lies in my surface pores. Hard at work in the catalytic converters of modern cars, I can potentially save the planet from harmful hydrocarbon emissions.

- ● Density   12.023 g/cm³
- ● Melting point 1,554.9°C (2,830.82°F)
- ● Boiling point 2,963°C (5,365°F)

Pd

Date of discovery: 1803

47 Silver

■ The Transition Elements

* ✹ Symbol: Ag
* ✹ Atomic number: 47
* ✹ Atomic weight: 107.87
* ✹ Color: Silver
* ✹ Standard state: Solid at 25°C (77°F)
* ✹ Classification: Metallic

I'm as lustrous and luscious as a shining star! Whether made into money, jewelry, or candlesticks, I have always been coveted for my short-lived shininess. But I always lose out to gold because I can't help forming silver sulfide when I come into contact with air. This forms a layer of black tarnish that needs to be cleaned off.

I'm soft and easy to work with. Dentists use a little of me in so-called silver fillings (which are really mostly mercury). My conductivity is first-rate, making me popular in electrical devices. As light-sensitive silver bromide and silver iodide compounds, I was coated onto celluloid film, capturing photos and movies for the "silver screen," but digital cameras have killed off color film. Perhaps I'll become more famous for my antibacterial properties.

Earliest known use: c. 3000 B.C.

* ● Density — 10.490 g/cm³
* ● Melting point 961.78°C (1,763.2°F)
* ● Boiling point 2,162°C (3,924°F)

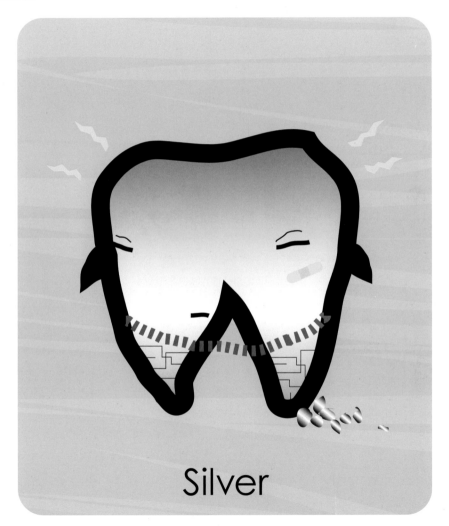

Silver

48 Cadmium

■ The Transition Elements

- ✹ Symbol: Cd
- ✹ Atomic number: 48
- ✹ Atomic weight: 112.41
- ✹ Color: Bluish silver-gray
- ✹ Standard state: Solid at 25°C (77°F)
- ✹ Classification: Metallic

Just another gray, shiny transition metal, you might think. I'm a superstable element, which means that when I'm mixed into steel, or used to plate it, the steel doesn't corrode. Boor-ring! But wait—beneath my bog standard exterior, I'm a flamboyant show-off. I've got swagger!

You see, when my atoms combine with other atoms and molecules, I burst out in bright reds, wild yellows, and glorious greens. My compounds make great paints. The famous artist Monet used to swear by my "cadmium yellow"! I also team up with nickel in rechargeable batteries. Like most braggers, too much of me will make you sick. Like mercury and lead, I tend to build up in the body if I make my way into water supplies and the food chain. This is why it's so important to recycle your batteries properly!

Date of discovery: 1817

- ● Density   8.65 g/cm³
- ● Melting point 321.07°C (609.93°F)
- ● Boiling point   767°C (1,413°F)

Cd

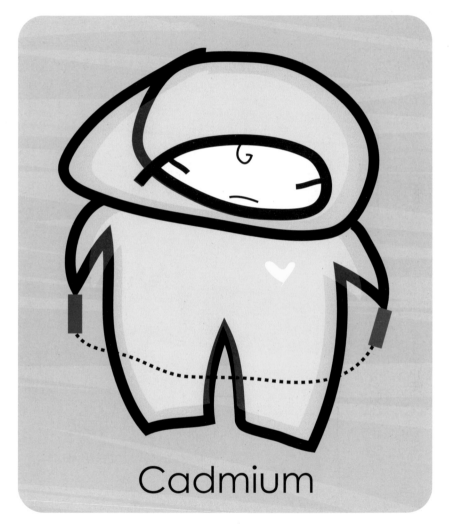

Cadmium

63

72 **Hafnium**

■ The Transition Elements

- ❋ Symbol: Hf
- ❋ Atomic number: 72
- ❋ Atomic weight: 178.49
- ❋ Color: Shiny steel
- ❋ Standard state: Solid at 25°C (77°F)
- ❋ Classification: Metallic

It's what you do, not what you say that's important. I'm a rugged guy who mops up stray neutrons in the raging fires of nuclear reactors. Superalloys made with me are so strong and heat-resistant that they're used for space vehicles. Mixed with tungsten and carbon, I have the highest melting point of any known compound.

Hafnium

Date of discovery: 1922

Hf
- ● Density   13.31 g/cm³
- ● Melting point   2,233°C (4,051°F)
- ● Boiling point   4,603°C (8,317°F)

Tantalum 73

The Transition Elements ■

* Symbol: Ta
* Atomic number: 73
* Atomic weight: 180.95

* Color: Blue-gray
* Standard state: Solid at 25°C (77°F)
* Classification: Metallic

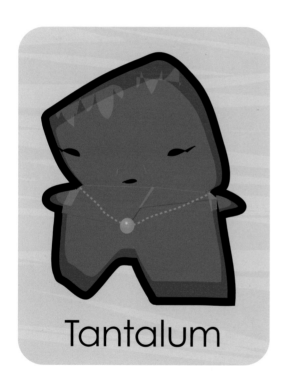

Tantalum

I'm one exotic dude! I come from the Democratic Republic of the Congo, in Africa, but you'll often find me much closer to home. I'm used to store, charge, and even out the current in almost every miniature electronic device you can think of. I'm totally corrosion-resistant and one of only two metals used for replacement body parts. Tantalizing!

Date of discovery: 1802

* Density   16.65 g/cm³
* Melting point   3,017°C (5,463°F)
* Boiling point   5,458°C (9,856°F)

Ta

65

74 **Tungsten**

■ The Transition Elements

* Symbol: W
* Atomic number: 74
* Atomic weight: 183.84

* Color: Gray-white
* Standard state: Solid at 25°C (77°F)
* Classification: Metallic

I'm one tough cookie, with the highest melting point of all metals and a boiling point close to 6,000°C (11,000°F), so you'll find me hard to liquefy and boil. In fact, you'll find me just plain harder than nails! I can be found protecting soldiers as bulletproof armor plating, and I bring light to the world in the filaments of lightbulbs.

Tungsten

Date of discovery: 1783

W
* Density   19.250 g/cm³
* Melting point 3,422°C (6,192°F)
* Boiling point 5,555°C (10,031°F)

Rhenium 75

The Transition Elements ▪

- ✸ Symbol: Re
- ✸ Atomic number: 75
- ✸ Atomic weight: 186.21

- ✸ Color: White-gray
- ✸ Standard state: Solid at 25°C (77°F)
- ✸ Classification: Metallic

Rhenium

Check me out! I am a truly rare, superexpensive substance. There's so little of me about, I was the last stable, naturally occurring element to be found. I am incredibly hard and heat-resistant. I just refuse to go soft, and this makes me a big player in jet-engine and rocket-booster superalloys. Here's a little-known fact: I was almost called "nipponium."

Date of discovery: 1925

- ● Density   21.02 g/cm³
- ● Melting point   3,186°C (5,767°F)
- ● Boiling point   5,596°C (10,105°F)

Re

67

76 Osmium

■ The Transition Elements

- ✹ Symbol: Os
- ✹ Atomic number: 76
- ✹ Atomic weight: 190.23

- ✹ Color: Faint silver-blue
- ✹ Standard state: Solid at 25°C (77°F)
- ✹ Classification: Metallic

Iridium and I battle it out for the title of densest element. I'm winning at the moment, but perhaps we should share the honors, since I'm always hanging out with him. Together, we're called osmiridium and are used for fancy pen nibs (we've sure got the *write* stuff). Many of my compounds are stinky—you could call me a "smell-ement!"

Osmium

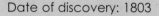
Date of discovery: 1803

Os:
- Density   22.61 g/cm³
- Melting point   3.033°C (5,491°F)
- Boiling point   5,012°C (9,054°F)

Iridium 77

The Transition Elements ■

* Symbol: Ir
* Atomic number: 77
* Atomic weight: 192.22

* Color: Silver-white
* Standard state: Solid at 25°C (77°F)
* Classification: Metallic

Iridium

I'm not exactly a colorful element, but I am definitely a slinky one! Substances made with me tend to shimmer and twinkle as if wearing a many-colored coat. I'm in the platinum family of tough, hard, brittle, and rare metals. Compared to me, platinum is plentiful, but if you look, you'll find me in the touch screens of cell phones and tablets.

Date of discovery: 1748

● Density   22.65 g/cm³
● Melting point 2,466°C (4,471°F)
● Boiling point 4,428°C (8,002°F)

Ir

78 **Platinum**

■ The Transition Elements

- ✶ Symbol: Pt
- ✶ Atomic number: 78
- ✶ Atomic weight: 195.08

- ✶ Color: Silver-white
- ✶ Standard state: Solid at 25°C (77°F)
- ✶ Classification: Metallic

I'm the last word in good taste. Rarer and even more expensive than gold, I am a bright, shiny metal found in South Africa and Russia. I am a real ladies' metal, used to make jewelry and adored for my endlessly fascinating sheen. Steadfast and dependable, I never lose my shine because I'm resistant to corrosion.

One of my most valuable uses, like so many of my fellow transition metals, is as a catalyst to get things started in industrial reactions. As steady as they come, my ability to remain unchanged made me the natural choice for the standard kilogram mass—*Le Grand Kilo*—that is stored in Paris, France, at the International Bureau of Weights and Measures. Another of my many and marvelous talents is being an essential component of anticancer drugs.

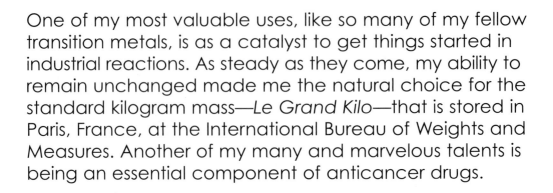

Date of discovery: 1735

- ● Density   21.090 g/cm³
- ● Melting point   1,768.3°C (3,214.9°F)
- ● Boiling point   3,825°C (6,917°F)

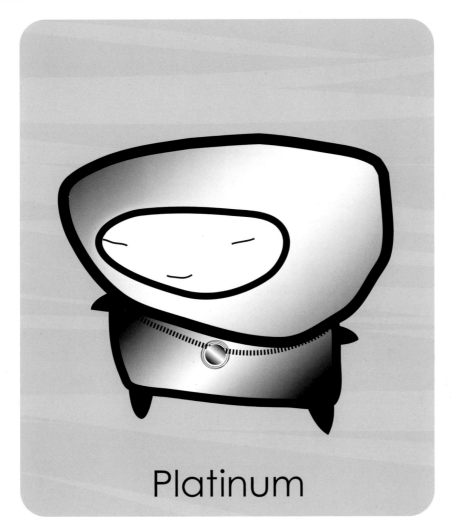

Platinum

79 **Gold**

■ The Transition Elements

✴ Symbol: Au
✴ Atomic number: 79
✴ Atomic weight: 196.97

✴ Color: Gold
✴ Standard state: Solid at 25°C (77°F)
✴ Classification: Metallic

I am not the rarest or the most expensive element, but I am the world's most wanted. I am the original gold-rush king, the ultimate attention seeker, and a bling party lover! At heart, I'm soft (for a metal), which makes me very easy to work with, and I can be polished to a high shine. My attraction lies in my resistance to corrosion (oxidation), meaning that I can be found in pure form inside Earth. I always remain a glistening temptation.

I am found in jewelry, in most electronic equipment (I'm a sparkling conductor of electricity), as crowns on teeth, in arthritis treatments, and, of course, as solid-gold bullion. My purity is measured in carats—24 carat is my purest form, but I can be alloyed (combined) with other metals to make 22-, 18-, 14-, and nine-carat gold.

Earliest known use: c. 3000 B.C.

● Density   19.300 g/cm³
● Melting point 1,064.18°C (1,947.52°F)
● Boiling point 2,856°C (5,173°F)

Gold

80 **Mercury**

■ The Transition Elements

- ✴ Symbol: Hg
- ✴ Atomic number: 80
- ✴ Atomic weight: 200.59
- ✴ Color: Silvery
- ✴ Standard state: Liquid at 25°C (77°F)
- ✴ Classification: Metallic

Quick and deadly, that's me. A sinister, silver-colored killer, I am a strange and stealthy liquid metal that easily vaporizes into toxic fumes. I put the "mad" in the Mad Hatter—hatmakers who used mercury nitrate for their work often succumbed to a strange delirium called "mercury madness." My ability to poison the brain is legendary and most of the forms I take are lethal.

I tend to build up inside the bodies of animals, especially in fish that swim in waters that are polluted by me. I attack the nervous systems of creatures that eat the contaminated fish. Alchemists mistakenly thought they could use me to turn base metals into gold, and I was once widely used in mining, for tooth fillings, and in thermometers. Health and safety rules now restrict my use and I'm difficult to find.

Earliest known use: c. 1500 B.C.

- ● Density   13.534 g/cm³
- ● Melting point −38.83°C (−37.89°F)
- ● Boiling point 356.73°C (674.11°F)

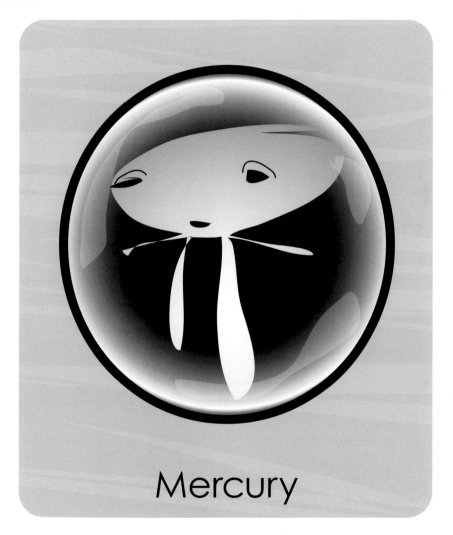

Mercury

CHAPTER 4
The Boron Elements

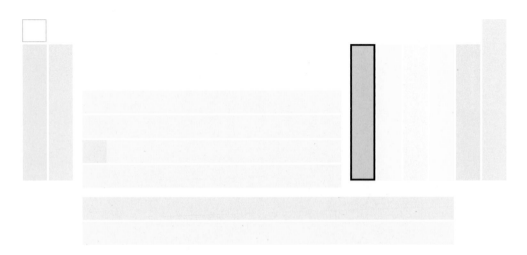

This ragtag group of elements is the periodic table's dysfunctional family. They don't gel together—some of them aren't even the same type of substance! Lonely, odd-man-out boron is an unusual powdery nonmetal, while the rest are soft, silvery, and weak metals. At the top of the group, these metals aren't especially metallic, but the farther down the group you go, the more like metals the members get. The boron elements are reactive enough to form many different compounds and are found in nature as various minerals and ores.

| 5  **B** BORON | 13  **Al** ALUMINUM | 31  **Ga** GALLIUM |
| 49 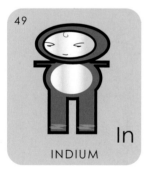 **In** INDIUM | 81  **Tl** THALLIUM | 113  **Uut** ELEMENT 113 |

5 Boron

The Boron Elements

* Symbol: B
* Atomic number: 5
* Atomic weight: 10.81
* Color: Brownish-black
* Standard state: Solid at 25°C (77°F)
* Classification: Nonmetallic

People make fun of my name and call me "Boring Boron." Okay, so I'm not flamboyant and I dress in brown and black, but I'm really nice to have around. I'm a facilitator and a helpful element that gets things done—a self-starter, if I can be so bold.

Whether helping out in glass manufacturing, in detergents, or—in my guise as borax and boric acid—coaxing along chemical reactions in industry, I'm on the case. My compound boron nitrate is almost as hard as diamond.

Far from tedious, you can think of me as a maverick. I am literally the "black-brown sheep" of the boron element family, since I'm the only nonmetal among my metallic friends.

Date of discovery: 1808

* Density   2.460 g/cm³
* Melting point   2,076°C (3,769°F)
* Boiling point   3,927°C (7,101°F)

Boron

13 Aluminum

■ The Boron Elements

* Symbol: Al
* Atomic number: 13
* Atomic weight: 26.982
* Color: Silver-gray
* Standard state: Solid at 25°C (77°F)
* Classification: Metallic

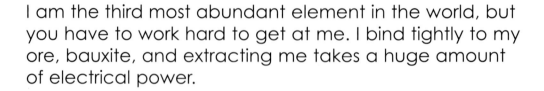

I'm light on my feet, and my pocket-battleship strength has made me a powerhouse metal. I'm a featherweight who literally punches above my weight! I offer a superior blend of strength and lightness—you can make me into airplanes, "tin" cans, and foil.

I am the third most abundant element in the world, but you have to work hard to get at me. I bind tightly to my ore, bauxite, and extracting me takes a huge amount of electrical power.

My salts help purify water by causing impurities to drop out of solutions as solids, but they have been linked to poisoning. When I show up in tap water, I have turned people's hair green and caused brain disorders.

Date of discovery: 1825

● Density   2.700 g/cm³
● Melting point 660.32°C (1,220.58°F)
● Boiling point   2,519°C (4,566°F)

Aluminum

31 Gallium

■ The Boron Elements

- ✳ Symbol: Ga
- ✳ Atomic number: 31
- ✳ Atomic weight: 69.723
- ✳ Color: Silvery
- ✳ Standard state: Solid at 25°C (77°F)
- ✳ Classification: Metallic

For a tough, shiny metal, I'm a little soppy—I melt so easily that I become liquid in your hand. For the same reason, I'm a bit of a joker. You see, a teaspoon made of me will literally disappear when used to stir tea! Paired with arsenic, I'm a hit in the electronics industry and may even come to rival silicon for the top spot.

Gallium

Date of discovery: 1875

- ● Density 5.904 g/cm³
- ● Melting point 29.76°C (85.57°F)
- ● Boiling point 2,204°C (3,999°F)

Indium 49

The Boron Elements

* Symbol: In
* Atomic number: 49
* Atomic weight: 114.82

* Color: Shiny silver
* Standard state: Solid at 25°C (77°F)
* Classification: Metallic

Indium

I'm one class act, baby, believe me. A soft, sticky metal with a low melting point, when I team up with oxygen (and tin) I come into my own. Indium tin oxide is see-through and conducts electricity. It is used for solar cells and LCD displays, touch screen technology for cell phones, and window demisters for cars.

Date of discovery: 1864

* Density   7.31 g/cm³
* Melting point 156.6°C (313.88°F)
* Boiling point 2,072°C (3,762°F)

In

81 **Thallium**

■ The Boron Elements

* ✹ Symbol: Tl
* ✹ Atomic number: 81
* ✹ Atomic weight: 204.38

* ✹ Color: Dullish gray
* ✹ Standard state: Solid at 25°C (77°F)
* ✹ Classification: Metallic

I am the duck-billed platypus of the elements —with properties I've borrowed from silver, platinum, and lead, I look as if I've been cobbled together. Colorless, odorless, and tasteless, I'm almost impossible to detect, and I'm poisonous to boot. Once I'm in your body, I mimic potassium, slip inside your cells, and wreak havoc.

Thallium

Date of discovery: 1861

Tl

- ● Density   11.85 g/cm³
- ● Melting point   304°C (579°F)
- ● Boiling point   1,473°C (2,683°F)

Element 113 113
The Boron Elements

- ✷ Symbol: Uut
- ✷ Atomic number: 113
- ✷ Atomic weight: 284.18

- ✷ Color: Unknown
- ✷ Standard state: Solid at 25°C (77°F)
- ✷ Classification: Metallic

Element 113

Things have gotten heavy around here, man. I was discovered in 2004, and I still have no name. No sooner am I brought to life in the dark of a particle-accelerator tube than I start winking out of existence: 20 seconds, and I'm half gone. Formed when element 115 decays, I can also be made by smashing bismuth and zinc nuclei together.

Date of discovery: 2004

- ● Density   16 g/cm³
- ● Melting point   unknown
- ● Boiling point   unknown

Uut

85

CHAPTER 5
The Carbon Elements

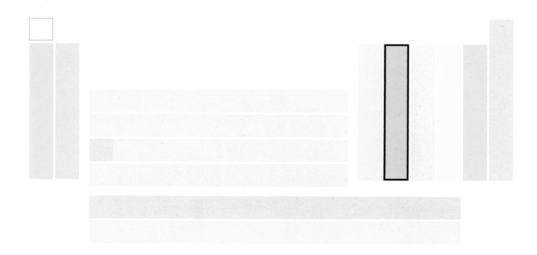

Unpredictability hangs like a magician's cloak over this group of tricky chemicals. They have very few striking similarities. Carbon is a hard (and even sometimes transparent) nonmetal, while tin and lead are softer metals. Like Group 13, the carbon elements get more metallic toward the bottom of the table. The members form a bewildering variety of different compounds, so perhaps it would be better to consider each element as an individual, rather than as part of a collection of like-minded substances.

6

C

CARBON

14

Si

SILICON

32

Ge

GERMANIUM

50

Sn

TIN

82

Pb

LEAD

114

Fl

FLEROVIUM

6 Carbon

■ The Carbon Elements

* ✳ Symbol: C
* ✳ Atomic number: 6
* ✳ Atomic weight: 12.011
* ✳ Color: Black
* ✳ Standard state: Solid at 25°C (77°F)
* ✳ Classification: Nonmetallic

Hah-yah! Wherever you look, I'm there. Like a ninja, there's no escaping me! A master of the black arts, I'm a stealthy element and can morph into many forms—black charcoal, hard and brilliant diamond, slippery graphite, wonder material graphene, and lovely buckminsterfullerene balls. My ability to form several types of chemical bonds with myself means I can whip myself into all sorts of shapes. With so many different guises, there's a whole branch of "organic" chemistry devoted to me.

I form the bulk of all living matter. Almost everything you eat—fats, sugars, and fiber—is a carbon-based compound. I move around the food chain in what's called "the carbon cycle." I'm released from food when you breathe and in your body waste, absorbed by plants, and then eaten again.

No known date of discovery

* ● Density 2.267 g/cm³
* ● Melting point 3,500°C (6,400.6°F)
* ● Boiling point 4,027°C (7,281°F)

C

Carbon

14 Silicon

The Carbon Elements

* Symbol: Si
* Atomic number: 14
* Atomic weight: 28.085
* Color: Glassy off-white
* Standard state: Solid at 25°C (77°F)
* Classification: Nonmetallic

My beguiling charms make computers run and power the digital age. Combined with boron or phosphorus, I become a semiconducting sorcerer. These special powers gave birth to the silicon chip and the Computer Age. Silicon Valley in California is named after me.

I take many different forms. As the second most abundant element on Earth, I crop up in sand, quartz, flint, and countless other minerals. As silicone (a long chain made up of me, oxygen, and organic chemicals), I'm in lubricants, adhesives, and body implants.

In glass, I'm perfectly clear. In quartz watches and clocks, I keep time, while as silica gel, I ensure that products are moisture-free. You'll find me inside sachets, packed inside boxes of electrical goods.

Date of discovery: 1824

● Density   2.330 g/cm³
● Melting point 1,414°C (2,577°F)
● Boiling point   2,900°C (5,252°F)

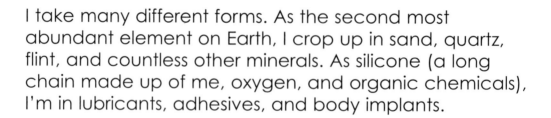

Silicon

32 Germanium

■ The Carbon Elements

- ✹ Symbol: Ge
- ✹ Atomic number: 32
- ✹ Atomic weight: 72.63
- ✹ Color: Shiny gray-white
- ✹ Standard state: Solid at 25°C (77°F)
- ✹ Classification: Metalloid

I am the granddaddy of the electronics industry. Poised somewhere in between a metal and a nonmetal, I have special abilities as a semiconductor. I was used in the very first transistors, but have now been replaced by silicon. Nonetheless, I make myself useful in fiber-optic cables, flashing info across the globe. Zap!

Germanium

Date of discovery: 1886

Ge:
- ● Density — 5.323 g/cm³
- ● Melting point — 938.9°C (1,720°F)
- ● Boiling point — 2,820°C (5,108°F)

Tin 50

The Carbon Elements

* Symbol: Sn
* Atomic number: 50
* Atomic weight: 118.71

* Color: Dull silver
* Standard state: Solid at 25°C (77°F)
* Classification: Metallic

Tin

I am too soft for my own good, and that's my problem. I melt at a low temperature (for a metal), and below 13°C (55°F), I change from a solid into a crumbly powder. I get mixed with other metals to keep me in shape. (I'm only a thin coating on "tin" cans—they're actually made of aluminum or steel.) Mingled with copper, I make bronze.

Earliest known use: c. 3500 B.C.

* Density   7.310 g/cm³
* Melting point   231.93°C (449.47°F)
* Boiling point   2,602°C (4,716°F)

 Sn

82 Lead

■ The Carbon Elements

* ✸ Symbol: Pb
* ✸ Atomic number: 82
* ✸ Atomic weight: 207.2
* ✸ Color: Dull, dark gray
* ✸ Standard state: Solid at 25°C (77°F)
* ✸ Classification: Metallic

Soft and malleable, I'm so easy to work with that the ancient Romans used me for their water pipes. Over the years, I've gained a bad rep. My unfortunate ability to slip easily into the food chain—from pipes and cookware—means I'm regulated closely. But I am still used as a shield against x-rays, for roofing, and in stained glass.

Lead

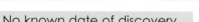

No known date of discovery

Pb:
● Density   11.340 g/cm³
● Melting point   327.46°C (621.43°F)
● Boiling point   1,749°C (3,180°F)

Flerovium 114
The Carbon Elements

* Symbol: Fl
* Atomic number: 114
* Atomic weight: 289.19

* Color: Unknown
* Standard state: Solid at 25°C (77°F)
* Classification: Metallic

Flerovium

Relatively new and something of a mystery, I'm usually made by getting plutonium and calcium nuclei to bond. While some of my forms last 60 seconds before breaking down—quite a long time in the heavy element world—most have speedier half-lives. I sit with the carbon family, but scientists think I could be more like a noble gas.

Date of discovery: 1998

● Density   14 g/cm³
● Melting point unknown
● Boiling point unknown

Fl

CHAPTER 6

The Nitrogen Elements

The "pnictogens" (*say* nick-toe-jens), as they are sometimes (but rarely) called, are an ancient and alchemical group with an odd collection of properties to boot. This group is a real mishmash of matter—there are metals, nonmetals, and strange metalloids; several elements exist in two different guises; and there's a mixture of gases and solids thrown in for good measure. Like most groups in the periodic table, the elements of Group 15 get increasingly metallic toward the base. Nitrogen is a colorless gas, while bismuth is a brittle metal.

7

N

NITROGEN

15

P

PHOSPHORUS

33

As

ARSENIC

51

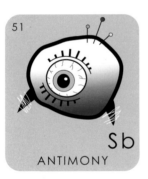

Sb

ANTIMONY

83

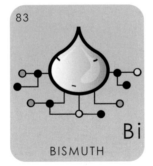

Bi

BISMUTH

115

Uup

ELEMENT 115

7 Nitrogen

The Nitrogen Elements

* Symbol: N
* Atomic number: 7
* Atomic weight: 14.007

* Color: None
* Standard state: Gas at 25°C (77°F)
* Classification: Nonmetallic

On first impression I'm a regular sort, but I've got an explosive temperament. You might hardly notice me, but I make up almost 80 percent of air, and I'm essential to plant life on Earth.

I'm normally a pretty unreactive gas, made up of two atoms of nitrogen (N_2). The triple bond between these two atoms is hard to break, and that is my hidden power. When my atoms form these bonds, they release massive amounts of energy. This makes many compounds that contain nitrogen potentially explosive!

I'm very easy to extract from air. I am a spectacular coolant in liquid form. At close to –200°C (–328°F), I will freeze almost anything that comes into contact with me.

Date of discovery: 1772

● Density   1.145 g/l
● Melting point   –210.1°C (–346.18°F)
● Boiling point   –195.79°C (–320.42°F)

Nitrogen

15 **Phosphorus**

The Nitrogen Elements

* Symbol: P
* Atomic number: 15
* Atomic weight: 30.974

* Color: Black, red, or white
* Standard state: Solid at 25°C (77°F)
* Classification: Nonmetallic

Like anything intriguing, I'm hard to pin down. I'm a Dr. Jekyll and Mr. Hyde element—essential to life, yet wickedly dangerous at the same time—a chameleon that appears in black, red, or white. I play a pivotal part in the DNA molecule and in the body, but I can be deadly. My white form ignites in air and even burns underwater! I can inflict terrible burns, and sadly I was used for that purpose in World War II. I am a central element in sarin—a lethal nerve gas that has been used in a number of terrorist attacks.

Arguably my most important use is in fertilizers. I am also used in many foods as phosphoric acid (an acidifying agent). You can find me in any bottle of cola, which is why you can use this soft drink as a rust remover.

Date of discovery: 1669

● Density   1.823 g/cm³
● Melting point 44.2°C (111.6°F)
● Boiling point   277°C (531°F)

Phosphorus

33 Arsenic

■ The Nitrogen Elements

* ✹ Symbol: As
* ✹ Atomic number: 33
* ✹ Atomic weight: 74.922

* ✹ Color: Gray or yellow
* ✹ Standard state: Solid at 25°C (77°F)
* ✹ Classification: Metalloid

Make no mistake, I'm a deadly element and a master of disguise to boot! One minute I'm a gray-colored metal, the next a yellow-colored nonmetal. I wreak havoc in developing countries, where industrial pollution allows me to sneak into the drinking water. Contamination with me causes widespread health issues. Nasty!

Arsenic

Earliest known use: c. 1250

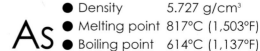

As:
* ● Density   5.727 g/cm³
* ● Melting point   817°C (1,503°F)
* ● Boiling point   614°C (1,137°F)

Antimony 51
The Nitrogen Elements

* Symbol: Sb
* Atomic number: 51
* Atomic weight: 121.76
* Color: Silver-gray
* Standard state: Solid at 25°C (77°F)
* Classification: Metalloid

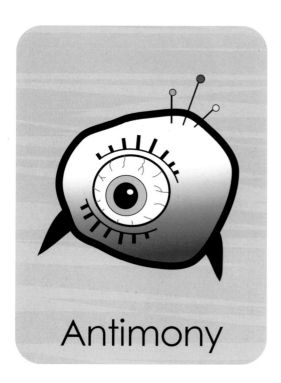

Antimony

A curious and ancient metalloid, I am often found attached to other elements. Keep an eye out for me— although I'm used in mascara, I can induce violent vomiting and certain death. Like my buddy arsenic, I used to be popular among those with murder in mind. Today I'm more often used to make alloys and semiconductors.

No known date of discovery

* Density   6.697 g/cm³
* Melting point   630.63°C (1,167.13°F)
* Boiling point   1,587°C (2,889°F)

 Sb

83 **Bismuth**

■ The Nitrogen Elements

* Symbol: Bi
* Atomic number: 83
* Atomic weight: 208.98
* Color: Silver-white
* Standard state: Solid at 25°C (77°F)
* Classification: Metallic

People tend to confuse me with tin or lead, which bugs me. I'm special, too! I am the heaviest nonradioactive element. Others may decay to form more durable elements giving off radiation, but I'm stable. Because I can easily turn into a liquid, I am used as part of fire-alarm systems. When I melt in intense heat, this triggers the alarms and water sprinklers.

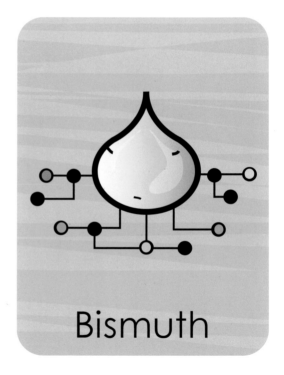

Bismuth

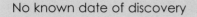

No known date of discovery

Bi

● Density 9.780 g/cm3
● Melting point 271.3°C (520.3°F)
● Boiling point 1,564°C (2,847°F)

Element 115 115

The Nitrogen Elements ■

- ✳ Symbol: Uup
- ✳ Atomic number: 115
- ✳ Atomic weight: 288.19

- ✳ Color: Unknown
- ✳ Standard state: Solid at 25°C (77°F)
- ✳ Classification: Metallic

Element 115

I've been around since 2004, and you won't catch me leaving the comfort of my particle accelerators. No sooner have calcium and americium cozied up (well, hammered together at eye-watering speeds) to make me than I'm falling apart again—in as little as 220 milliseconds! On the way out, I decay into element 113.

Discovered in 2004

- ● Density   13 g/cm³
- ● Melting point   unknown
- ● Boiling point   unknown

Uup

CHAPTER 7
The Oxygen Elements

In this neighborhood of the periodic table, the groups of elements are more like bunches of friends than family units. Nothing is truer for Group 16—it's a real mixed bag of solids, gases, nonmetals, metalloids, and even a radioactive metal—but the oxygen elements are a cosmopolitan crew that get involved in important industrial reactions and are vital to many life processes. They sport the unlikely name "the chalcogens," which means "ore formers," because in nature they are often found combined with metals.

8

O

OXYGEN

16

S

SULFUR

34

Se

SELENIUM

52

Te

TELLURIUM

84

Po

POLONIUM

116

Lv

LIVERMORIUM

8 Oxygen

The Oxygen Elements

- ✷ Symbol: O
- ✷ Atomic number: 8
- ✷ Atomic weight: 15.999
- ✷ Color: None
- ✷ Standard state: Gas at 25°C (77°F)
- ✷ Classification: Nonmetallic

Quiet and unassuming, I'm colorless, odorless, and tasteless. Some say I lack personality, but they don't recognize true greatness. I am the powerhouse behind most chemical reactions on Earth. Without *me*, you die.

I'm a gas made up of two atoms (O_2) that combines readily with other substances in "oxidation reactions" in order to release energy. When you breathe me in, I slip into your bloodstream. Once I'm inside your body, every single cell uses me to fuel life-sustaining chemical reactions.

I am also found in teams of three atoms (O_3) as a gas known as ozone. When I take this form high up in the sky, I protect Earth from the Sun's harmful ultraviolet rays.

Date of discovery: 1774

- ● Density   1.308 g/l
- ● Melting point −218.3°C (−360.9°F)
- ● Boiling point −182.9°C (−297.2°F)

Oxygen

16 Sulfur

The Oxygen Elements

* Symbol: S
* Atomic number: 16
* Atomic weight: 32.065
* Color: Pale yellow
* Standard state: Solid at 25°C (77°F)
* Classification: Nonmetallic

Sweetly smiling and dressed in pale yellow, I look as harmless as a lemon tart, but I have a wicked side. . . I am a fun-loving prankster that loves to unleash bad smells. My most vile whiffs include rotten eggs and foul skunky odors. But it's not really me—it's my compounds that stink—hydrogen sulfide (H_2S) is the most likely culprit.

I was once known as "brimstone" and featured in fiery descriptions of hell. This reputation probably comes from the fact that I ooze from the pores of active volcanoes. When exposed to oxygen and heated, I spontaneously combust with a bright and intense light. These qualities make me an important part of gunpowder. I also cause acid rain. I am an essential element in sulfuric acid—a chemical used to make a variety of other substances.

No known date of discovery

* Density   1.960 g/cm^3
* Melting point   115.21°C (239.38°F)
* Boiling point   444.72°C (832.5°F)

Sulfur

34 **Selenium**

The Oxygen Elements

- ☀ Symbol: Se
- ☀ Atomic number: 34
- ☀ Atomic weight: 78.96
- ☀ Color: Gray
- ☀ Standard state: Solid at 25°C (77°F)
- ☀ Classification: Nonmetallic

My name comes from the Greek word *selene*, meaning "moon"—I am a remote and mysterious element. A lack of me in your diet gives you Keshan disease, which causes heart muscle failure. But when animals eat me concentrated in plants such as vetch (aka "locoweed"), I make them stagger around as if they were drunk!

Selenium

Date of discovery: 1817

Se
- ● Density   4.819 g/cm³
- ● Melting point 221°C (430°F)
- ● Boiling point   685°C (1,265°F)

Tellurium 52
The Oxygen Elements

* Symbol: Te
* Atomic number: 52
* Atomic weight: 127.60

* Color: Silver-gray
* Standard state: Solid at 25°C (77°F)
* Classification: Semimetal

Tellurium

Although useful in electronics, I'm a real problem child. I've been a puzzle since day one, and identifying and classifying me has been a dizzying quandary. As a corrupting influence, I am without equal. I'm about the only compound that can touch the spotless gold. In the body I cause extremely bad breath, as well as horrible body odor.

Date of discovery: 1783

● Density   6.240 g/cm³
● Melting point 449.51°C (841.12°F)
● Boiling point 988°C (1,810°F)

Te

113

84 **Polonium**

■ The Oxygen Elements

- ✹ Symbol: Po
- ✹ Atomic number: 84
- ✹ Atomic weight: 208.98
- ✹ Color: Silvery
- ✹ Standard state: Solid at 25°C (77°F)
- ✹ Classification: Metallic

I am a radioactive fellow, discovered by the famous scientist Marie Curie. I was her first new element and she named me after her homeland, Poland. Well, that's a heartwarming tale, but aside from being used to heat spacecraft, there's little that's kind or cozy about me. I have a reputation for being a secret weapon that's used for killing spies.

Polonium

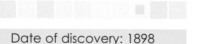

Date of discovery: 1898

Po
- ● Density   9.196 g/cm³
- ● Melting point   254°C (489°F)
- ● Boiling point   962°C (1,764°F)

Livermorium 116
The Oxygen Elements

* Symbol: Lv
* Atomic number: 116
* Atomic weight: 293

* Color: Unknown
* Standard state: Solid at 25°C (77°F)
* Classification: Metallic

Livermorium

Glory-seeking scientists will stop at nothing to discover new elements. I'm a new one, made by crashing together calcium and curium nuclei. It's a complex and costly process that requires exceptional facilities. It's "Big Science," and only four labs can do it—RIKEN in Japan, Berkeley in the U.S., Dubna in Russia, and Darmstadt in Germany.

Date of discovery: 2000

* Density   11.2 g/cm³
* Melting point unknown
* Boiling point unknown

Lv

CHAPTER 8
The Halogen Elements

We're back in the family zone again, but this side of the periodic table is where the nonmetal elements live, separated from the metals to their left. The halogens are a close-knit group of lively, strongly colored nonmetals. They are a feisty bunch that will react violently with metals to form salts ("halogen" means "salt giver"). The elements at the top of Group 17 are yellow and green toxic gases, but as you move down through the group, things get progressively darker. . .

9  F	17  Cl	35  Br
FLUORINE	CHLORINE	BROMINE
53  I	85 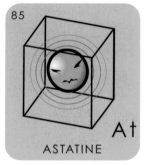 At	117  Uus
IODINE	ASTATINE	ELEMENT 117

9 Fluorine

■ The Halogen Elements

✷ Symbol: F
✷ Atomic number: 9
✷ Atomic weight: 18.998

✷ Color: Pale yellow-green
✷ Standard state: Gas at 25°C (77°F)
✷ Classification: Nonmetallic

I'm a doer—a lively package set off by the perfect Hollywood smile. I am added to drinking water to help protect your teeth, and I form lots of really useful compounds—such as Teflon®, the famous nonstick coating. Running through all of the wonderful things I do is a competitive streak. I am superreactive, and I will take an electron from almost any atom or molecule in order to complete my set. This is just one of the reasons why I'm so usable and form so many nifty compounds.

The only blot on my record is my involvement with CFCs (chlorofluorocarbons)—the compounds that have done so much damage to Earth's ozone layer. I don't like to talk about it. My invasive choking smell signals my true toxic nature. So, be warned!

Date of discovery: 1886

● Density   1.553 g/l
● Melting point −219.62°C (−363.32°F)
● Boiling point −188.12°C (−306.62°F)

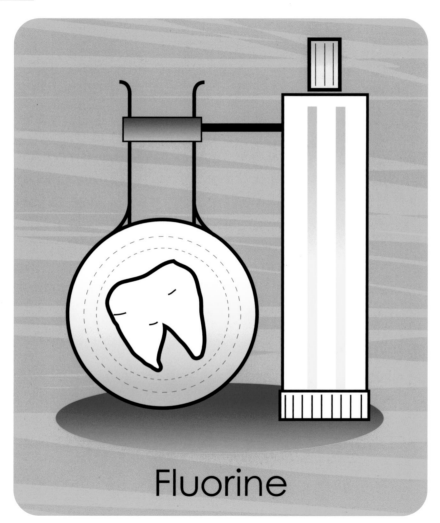

Fluorine

17 Chlorine

■ The Halogen Elements

✸ Symbol: Cl
✸ Atomic number: 17
✸ Atomic weight: 35.45

✸ Color: Green
✸ Standard state: Gas at 25°C (77°F)
✸ Classification: Nonmetallic

You've gotta give me some respect! I'm a mean, green, killing machine. One of the halogen gang, I'm a toxic gas with a horrible history. I first became a terrifying chemical weapon during World War I, when my sinister, choking fumes killed thousands of people. I'm even bad enough to battle bacteria in the toilet bowl! But I can also keep you safe from waterborne diseases, such as cholera and typhoid fever. Adding small amounts of me to drinking water supplies has saved millions of people's lives.

Usually obtained from common salt, you'll find me in all sorts of places, from saltshakers to swimming pools (where I keep the water bacteria-free). I have also been used as an especially un-environmentally friendly pesticide called DDT and am associated with CFCs (see fluorine).

Date of discovery: 1774

● Density   2.898 g/l
● Melting point −101.5°C (−150.7°F)
● Boiling point   −34.04°C (−29.27°F)

Chlorine

35 **Bromine**

■ The Halogen Elements

✳ Symbol: Br
✳ Atomic number: 35
✳ Atomic weight: 79.904

✳ Color: Orangish-brown
✳ Standard state: Liquid at 25°C (77°F)
✳ Classification: Nonmetallic

I am a regal element with a long history. One of only two liquids in the periodic table (the other is mercury), I was used in the royal dye of the ancient Roman Empire— "Tyrian purple." It is made from crushed seashells, and emperors and members of the imperial family wore me proudly to show everyone else how important they were.

Today I am extracted from seawater, and as an element, you'll find me to be a pungent-smelling, red-brown, volatile liquid. I'm ashamed to say that my name comes from the Greek word *bromos*, meaning "stench."

Until recently, doctors used my salts to suppress mental activity in disturbed patients, but not anymore, since their toxic nature has been revealed.

Date of discovery: 1826

● Density   3.1028 g/cm³
● Melting point   −7.3°C (19°F)
● Boiling point   59°C (138°F)

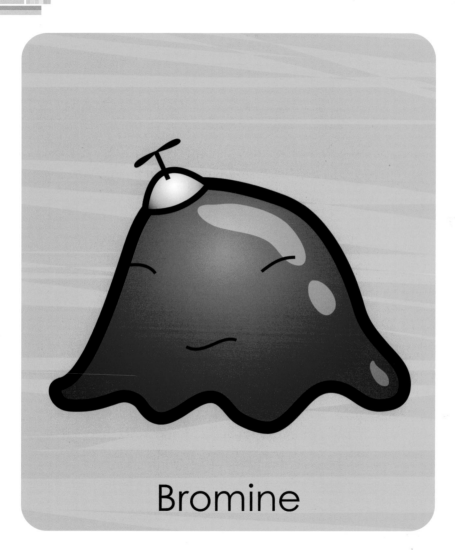

Bromine

53 Iodine

■ The Halogen Elements

* Symbol: I
* Atomic number: 53
* Atomic weight: 126.90

* Color: Shiny black
* Standard state: Solid at 25°C (77°F)
* Classification: Nonmetallic

I am a shiny black solid, but at room temperature I can change into a purplish gas without stopping to become a liquid. That's called "sublimation."

You'll almost never see me alone—I hang out in pairs as a gas (I_2). I am deadly to bacteria when I'm in a solution. I am a yellow-brown liquid that stings like heck when it gets dabbed onto a cut (although this may be the fault of the liquid alcohol). My antiseptic powers are so good that I'm used to clean up inside the body after surgery.

I've been sneaking into people's diets for many years disguised in table salt, but that's a good thing—I help eliminate the horrible swellings of the neck that used to affect people who didn't have enough of me inside their bodies.

Date of discovery: 1811

● Density   4.940 g/cm³
● Melting point   113.7°C (236.66°F)
● Boiling point   184.3°C (363.7°F)

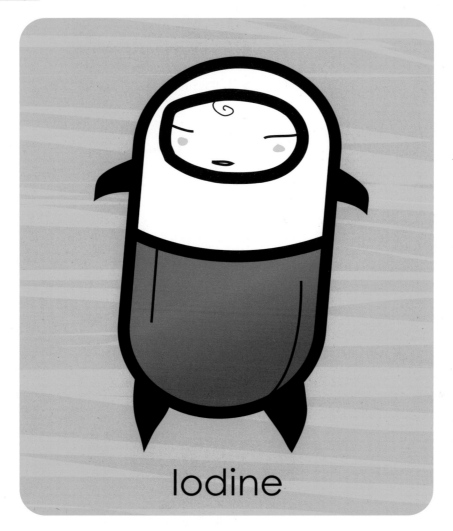

Iodine

85 Astatine

■ The Halogen Elements

- ✳ Symbol: At
- ✳ Atomic number: 85
- ✳ Atomic weight: 209.99
- ✳ Color: Unknown
- ✳ Standard state: Solid at 25°C (77°F)
- ✳ Classification: Nonmetallic

Sorry, I must rush. I've just got to pop! You see, I'm superradioactive and I don't hang around, if I can help it. I have a half-life of just eight hours. I'm a rarer than rare element —no sooner have I formed by the radioactive decay of a heavier element than I break down. They even gave me a name that means "unstable"! Well, fancy that!

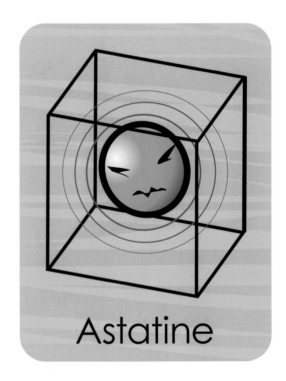

Astatine

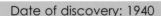

Date of discovery: 1940

At
- ● Density   6.4 g/cm³
- ● Melting point 302°C (576°F)
- ● Boiling point 230°C (446°F)

126

Element 117 117
The Halogen Elements ■

- ✳ Symbol: Uus
- ✳ Atomic number: 117
- ✳ Atomic weight: 294

- ✳ Color: Unknown
- ✳ Standard state: Solid at 25°C (77°F)
- ✳ Classification: Nonmetallic

Element 117

As recently as 2010, a joint team of Russian and U.S. scientists managed to make six atoms of me in a Russian laboratory. This makes me the element with the fewest number of atoms ever seen! I should be like the rest of the halogens, but first my discovery needs to be checked to see if it is genuine. Well, I ask you, the nerve of it!

Date of discovery: 2010

- ● Density   7.2 g/cm³
- ● Melting point unknown
- ● Boiling point   unknown

Uus

CHAPTER 9

Group 18

The Noble Gases

The far right of the table is the classy neighborhood, for here lives the periodic table's royal family—the so-called "noble gases." This group is largely resistant to chemical reactions, seemingly above mixing or slumming it with the rest of the elements. They were once called the "inert gases," meaning completely unreactive, but this isn't entirely true—some of them have been caught in clandestine clinches with other elements. They're not even that rare either—we now know that they all float around in the atmosphere, alone and aloof.

2

He

HELIUM

10

Ne

NEON

18

Ar

ARGON

36

Kr

KRYPTON

54

Xe

XENON

86

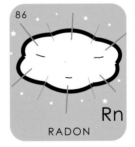

Rn

RADON

118

Uuo

ELEMENT 118

2 Helium

■ The Noble Gases

- ✳ Symbol: He
- ✳ Atomic number: 2
- ✳ Atomic weight: 4.0026
- ✳ Color: None
- ✳ Standard state: Gas at 25°C (77°F)
- ✳ Classification: Nonmetallic

I prefer my own company, thank you very much. Some call me aloof, but I'm happy not to mix with the riffraff of the periodic table. I am a "noble" gas—the very first. I am completely inert, with no color, taste, or smell. I am also known as a party prankster. Gulp me from a birthday balloon, and your voice will get all squeaky!

I am produced in massive stars such as the Sun, where four hydrogen atoms fuse together, releasing enormous amounts of energy. On Earth, my nucleus is one of the products of radioactive decay—the alpha particle.

My main uses are in weather balloons and airships—which need my lofty, lighter-than-air properties—and in welding, which requires an inert, unreactive atmosphere.

Date of discovery: 1895

- ● Density   0.164 g/l
- ● Melting point −272.2°C (−458°F)
- ● Boiling point   −268.93°C (−452.07°F)

Helium

10 **Neon**

■ The Noble Gases

* Symbol: Ne
* Atomic number: 10
* Atomic weight: 20.180

* Color: None
* Standard state: Gas at 25°C (77°F)
* Classification: Nonmetallic

I must be the funkiest element around. My name is derived from the Greek word *neos*, which means "new." (Maybe any new element could have been christened this way, but I think it suits me very well.) Things really get going when I become excited by electrical energy— my electrons zap and zing and make me emit bright, brilliant, and stunningly colored red light. When other elements are stirred into the mix, I can produce all the colors of the rainbow. This is how neon lights are made.

Even though I am found in something as common as air, I am a member of the periodic table's aristocracy—the noble gases. I keep myself to myself. I am a colorless, odorless, and tasteless gas, and there is virtually nothing that I will react with.

Date of discovery: 1898

● Density   0.825 g/l
● Melting point   −248.59°C (−415.46°F)
● Boiling point   −246.08°C (−410.94°F)

Neon

18 Argon
■ The Noble Gases

✳ Symbol: Ar
✳ Atomic number: 18
✳ Atomic weight: 39.948

✳ Color: None
✳ Standard state: Gas at 25°C (77°F)
✳ Classification: Nonmetallic

Bone idle and basically lazy, I'm totally lackluster—an odorless, colorless, and tasteless gas. I'm renowned for my unwillingness and inability to react with anything at all, but this can be a good thing—I am used as an "inert atmosphere" in potentially dangerous jobs, such as arc welding, when oxygen must be excluded in order to avoid explosions. I am also sometimes used in lightbulbs. You can even find me between the panes of some windows because I am such a poor conductor of heat.

As the third most abundant gas in Earth's atmosphere, I'm extracted from liquid air. Because I am produced when the radioactive isotope potassium-40 decays, my presence in the atmosphere is increasing with time.

Date of discovery: 1894

● Density   1.633 g/l
● Melting point −189.3°C (−308.7°F)
● Boiling point   −185.8°C (−302.4°F)

Argon

36 Krypton

■ The Noble Gases

- ✷ Symbol: Kr
- ✷ Atomic number: 36
- ✷ Atomic weight: 83.798
- ✷ Color: None
- ✷ Standard state: Gas at 25°C (77°F)
- ✷ Classification: Nonmetallic

I'm elusive to say the least! My name, from the Greek *kryptos*, means "hidden," and it is aptly chosen. I'm almost completely unreactive, colorless, odorless, and tasteless, and I'm only present in the atmosphere in vanishingly small amounts. Don't confuse me with the fictional home planet of Superman and the source of his nemesis—kryptonite!

Krypton

Date of discovery: 1898

Kr
- ● Density   3.425 g/l
- ● Melting point   −157.36°C (−251.25°F)
- ● Boiling point   −153.22°C (−243.8°F)

The Noble Gases ■

* Symbol: Xe
* Atomic number: 54
* Atomic weight: 131.29

* Color: None
* Standard state: Gas at 25°C (77°F)
* Classification: Nonmetallic

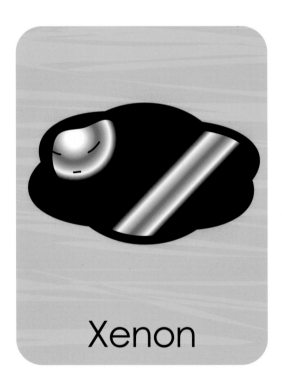

Xenon

I'm one bright fellow, I can tell you. As far as the noble gases go, I'm a bit of a tease and can actually be persuaded to make chemical compounds. So humph to the rest of those stuffed shirts! I make arc lamps so fantastically brilliant that they are used in IMAX movie projectors and the headlights of fancy automobiles.

Date of discovery: 1898

● Density   5.894 g/l
● Melting point   −111.7°C (−169.1°F)
● Boiling point   −108°C (−162°F)

Xe

137

86 **Radon**

■ The Noble Gases

* Symbol: Rn
* Atomic number: 86
* Atomic weight: 222.02

* Color: None
* Standard state: Gas at 25°C (77°F)
* Classification: Nonmetallic

Like my other "noble" family members, I'm almost completely immune to chemical reactions, but I'm a much more sparky character than the rest. I give off harmful radioactive alpha particles, and, since I occur in granite, there is a concern that I may build up inside houses in granitic areas and pose a risk of lung cancer.

Radon

Date of discovery: 1900

Rn:
● Density — 9.074 g/l
● Melting point — −71°C (−96°F)
● Boiling point — −61.7°C (−79.1°F)

Element 118 118

The Noble Gases ■

* Symbol: Uuo
* Atomic number: 118
* Atomic weight: 294

* Color: Unknown
* Standard state: Gas at 25°C (77°F)
* Classification: Metallic

Element 118

I'm as synthetic as they come—the last element on today's periodic table menu. It's a really painstaking process to make superheavy elements like me. Heavy ions are crashed together for months in particle accelerators. Eventually, enough atoms are created to be detected—often as few as three or four of them!

Date of discovery: 2002

● Density   5.7 g/cm³
● Melting point   unknown
● Boiling point   unknown

Uuo

CHAPTER 10
The Lanthanoid Elements

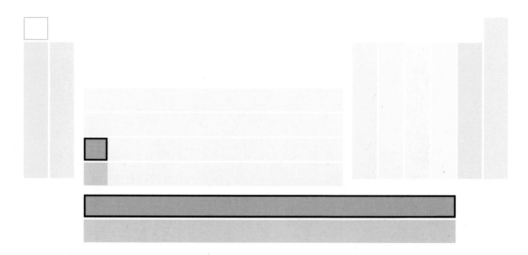

The lanthanoids are naturally occurring heavy metals. Grouped with the transition metals, yttrium and scandium, this weighty lot are often termed "rare earth" elements. Funny thing is, they're not all that rare, but are tricky to separate, which is why they were discovered later than many other naturally occurring elements. The plain-Jane lanthanoids have amazing magnetic- and light-amplifying properties—21st-century attributes that see them used in touch screens, wind turbines, batteries for cell phones and hybrid cars, as well as to date rocks from outer space.

57  La LANTHANUM	58  Ce CERIUM	59  Pr PRASEODYMIUM	60  Nd NEODYMIUM	61 Pm PROMETHIUM
62  Sm SAMARIUM	63 Eu EUROPIUM	64  Gd GADOLINIUM	65 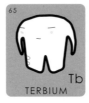 Tb TERBIUM	66  Dy DYSPROSIUM
67  Ho HOLMIUM	68 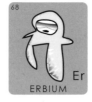 Er ERBIUM	69  Tm THULIUM	70  Yb YTTERBIUM	71  Lu LUTETIUM

57 Lanthanum

■ The Lanthanoid Elements

✳ Symbol: La
✳ Atomic number: 57
✳ Atomic weight: 138.91

✳ Color: Dull white
✳ Standard state: Solid at 25°C (77°F)
✳ Classification: Metallic

Peek-a-boo! I'm the boss of the lanthanoid crew. We're a close-knit bunch who like to hang out together in the same minerals. This makes us really difficult to separate chemically. In fact, my name comes from the Greek word *lanthanein* meaning "escape notice."

But for a deep-cover kind of guy, I've got some pretty flash tricks. Mixed with cerium and a dash of neodymium or praseodymium, I make a crazy flammable metal called "misch metal." It's used in flints for cigarette lighters and to make showers of sparks as a special effect for movies. Special glass incorporating my oxide compound makes high-quality, superaccurate lenses for cameras. My metal also forms an essential component of rechargeable nickel-metal hydride batteries in hybrid cars. All in all, I'm worth taking the trouble to find!

Date of discovery: 1839

● Density   6.162 g/l
● Melting point 920°C (1,688°F)
● Boiling point   3,470°C (6,278°F)

Lanthanum

58 Cerium

■ The Lanthanoid Elements

- ❋ Symbol: Ce
- ❋ Atomic number: 58
- ❋ Atomic weight: 140.12
- ❋ Color: Silver-white
- ❋ Standard state: Solid at 25°C (77°F)
- ❋ Classification: Metallic

You can call me Sparky! I'm a bright fellow, used in the flints of lighters and for dramatic sparkle effects in movies. Flakes of me spontaneously burst into flame—things certainly brighten up when I'm around! I'm on a mission to save the planet: tiny nanoparticles of my oxide are added to diesel fuel, to clean up its dirty exhaust emissions.

Cerium

Date of discovery: 1803

Ce
- ● Density   6.689 g/cm³
- ● Melting point   795°C (1,463°F)
- ● Boiling point   3,360°C (6,080°F)

Praseodymium 59
The Lanthanoid Elements ■

* ✷ Symbol: Pr
* ✷ Atomic number: 59
* ✷ Atomic weight: 140.91

* ✷ Color: Gray-whitish
* ✷ Standard state: Solid at 25°C (77°F)
* ✷ Classification: Metallic

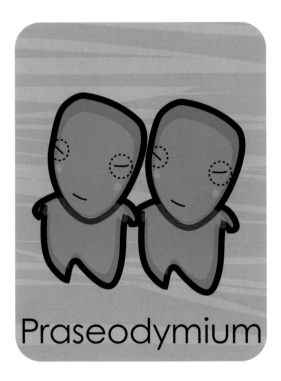

Praseodymium

Despite my flamboyant name, I'm really a bashful element in a shy group. I'm one of the elements classed as "rare earths." We are really similar to each other (which is why we have our own special row in the periodic table). You'll find me in the "didymium" glasses that shield glassblowers' eyes and the bright lights of movie projectors. Blinding!

Date of discovery: 1885

* ● Density   6.640 g/cm³
* ● Melting point   935°C (1,715°F)
* ● Boiling point   3,290°C (5,954°F)

Pr

60 **Neodymium**

■ The Lanthanoid Elements

- ✳ Symbol: Nd
- ✳ Atomic number: 60
- ✳ Atomic weight: 144.24
- ✳ Color: Dull silver
- ✳ Standard state: Solid at 25°C (77°F)
- ✳ Classification: Metallic

I am the great attractor—the element with the magnetic personality! Permanent magnets made with me (plus iron and boron) are thousands of times stronger than any other. You'll find me in the vibrating parts of your cell phone, in microphones and loudspeakers, in the electric motors of hybrid cars, in oil filters, and in computer hard disks.

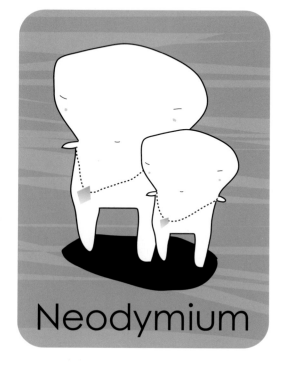

Neodymium

Nd:
- ● Density   6.8 g/cm³
- ● Melting point   1,024°C (1,875°F)
- ● Boiling point   3,100°C (5,612°F)

Promethium 61
The Lanthanoid Elements ■

* Symbol: Pm
* Atomic number: 61
* Atomic weight: 144.91

* Color: Metallic
* Standard state: Solid at 25°C (77°F)
* Classification: Metallic

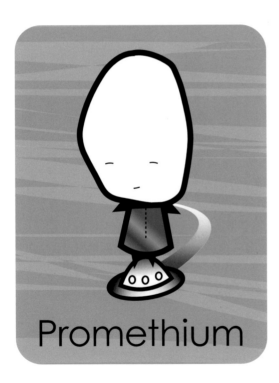

Promethium

They call me the Bringer of Fire—beat that for a name! I'm named after the Greek hero Prometheus, who stole fire from the gods and brought it to Earth, and even though I'm surrounded by stable elements, I'm unstable, radioactive, and dangerous! I'm used in industry to gauge the thickness of sheets of plastic, metal, or paper.

Date of discovery: 1945

* Density   7.264 g/cm³
* Melting point 1,100°C (2,012°F)
* Boiling point 3,000°C (5,432°F)

Pm

62 Samarium

■ The Lanthanoid Elements

- ✳ Symbol: Sm
- ✳ Atomic number: 62
- ✳ Atomic weight: 150.36

- ✳ Color: Lustrous silver
- ✳ Standard state: Solid at 25°C (77°F)
- ✳ Classification: Metallic

I'm a real do-gooder. You might call me the "Good Samarium" (geddit?). I'm used to date exotic rocks and in the control rods of nuclear reactors, 'cos I mop up stray neutrons. Mixed with cobalt, I make superstrong magnets that can be bashed around without losing any of their magnetism. They are used in electric guitar pickups and headphones.

Samarium

Date of discovery: 1879

 Sm :
- ● Density 7.353 g/cm³
- ● Melting point 1,072°C (1,962°F)
- ● Boiling point 1,803°C (3,277°F)

- ✴ Symbol: Eu
- ✴ Atomic number: 63
- ✴ Atomic weight: 151.96

- ✴ Color: Discolored silver
- ✴ Standard state: Solid at 25°C (77°F)
- ✴ Classification: Metallic

Europium

Suave and sophisticated, I'm quite the cosmopolitan European. Useful for all sorts of lighting, my compounds give off a spooky glow when light is shone on them. I help energy-efficient bulbs give out white light by combining my fluorescent red and blue glows. I also make a neat antiforgery strip on Euro banknotes. How very illuminating!

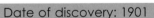

Date of discovery: 1901

- ● Density   5.244 g/cm³
- ● Melting point 826°C (1,519°F)
- ● Boiling point   1,527°C (2,781°F)

Eu

64 Gadolinium

■ The Lanthanoid Elements

- ✸ Symbol: Gd
- ✸ Atomic number: 64
- ✸ Atomic weight: 157.25
- ✸ Color: Silver-white
- ✸ Standard state: Solid at 25°C (77°F)
- ✸ Classification: Metallic

We lanthanoid elements like to keep things "plain vanilla." No alarms. No surprises. We are so similar to each other, chemically, yet I do my best to stand out from the rest. And I happen to excel in one area in particular: when injected into the body, my magnetic properties make it easy for an MRI machine to detect and pick out very fine details.

Gadolinium

Date of discovery: 1886

Gd :
- ● Density — 7.901 g/cm³
- ● Melting point — 1,312°C (2,394°F)
- ● Boiling point — 3,250°C (5,882°F)

150

Terbium 65

The Lanthanoid Elements ■

* ✹ Symbol: Tb
* ✹ Atomic number: 65
* ✹ Atomic weight: 158.93

* ✹ Color: Silver-white
* ✹ Standard state: Solid at 25°C (77°F)
* ✹ Classification: Metallic

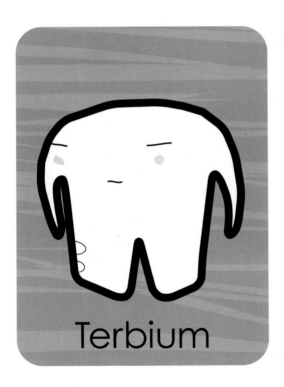

Terbium

Ter-bium or not ter-bium, that is the question! Well, let's find out. Stick me in a magnetic field and watch me writhe and wriggle! Compounds made with me have the strange ability to change their length when magnetized. This funky property is used to create "terbium-charged" devices that make any flat surface act as a speaker.

Date of discovery: 1843

* ● Density 8.19 g/cm³
* ● Melting point 1,356°C (2,473°F)
* ● Boiling point 3,230°C (5,846°F)

Tb

66 **Dysprosium**

■ The Lanthanoid Elements

* Symbol: Dy
* Atomic number: 66
* Atomic weight: 162.50

* Color: Bright silver
* Standard state: Solid at 25°C (77°F)
* Classification: Metallic

With such a downbeat name, it's no wonder I'm a moody soul. Dysprosium means "hard to get at," and I played hide-and-seek with chemists for almost 70 years. Since I'm so coy, I don't get used in many things. To be honest, there's not much I can do that one of my lanthanoid cousins can't do better or cheaper than me.

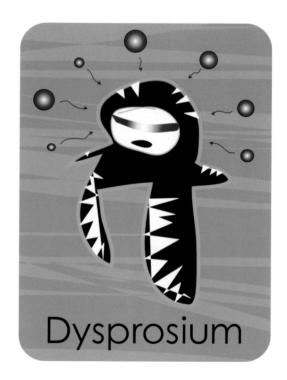

Dysprosium

Date of discovery: 1886

Dy
● Density   8.551 g/cm³
● Melting point   1,407°C (2,565°F)
● Boiling point   2,567°C (4,653°F)

Holmium 67

The Lanthanoid Elements

- Symbol: Ho
- Atomic number: 67
- Atomic weight: 164.93
- Color: Silver-white
- Standard state: Solid at 25°C (77°F)
- Classification: Metallic

"Holmium" your horses! I'm not magnetic in my own right, but put me in a magnetic field and I boost its strength like crazy. If you are a metal, you're going to find me irresistible! A small lump of me will soup up your run-of-the-mill bar magnet, and, used as the pole pieces in an MRI scanning machine, I'm stupendously powerful!

Date of discovery: 1878

- Density 8.795 g/cm^3
- Melting point 1,461°C (2,662°F)
- Boiling point 2,720°C (4,928°F)

Ho

68 **Erbium**

■ The Lanthanoid Elements

* Symbol: Er
* Atomic number: 68
* Atomic weight: 167.26

* Color: Shiny silver
* Standard state: Solid at 25°C (77°F)
* Classification: Metallic

My pretty pink ions have a magical talent with light—a small section of optical fiber doped with me "boosts" light traveling through it, so that it leaves brighter than it entered! When you use the telephone or go online, you use me to help deliver your data with blistering speed. I'm the secret behind the internet's success!

Erbium

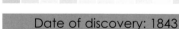

Date of discovery: 1843

Er

● Density   9.066 g/cm³
● Melting point   1,529°C (2,784°F)
● Boiling point   2,868°C (5,194°F)

154

✳ Symbol: Tm
✳ Atomic number: 69
✳ Atomic weight: 168.93

✳ Color: Silver-gray
✳ Standard state: Solid at 25°C (77°F)
✳ Classification: Metallic

Thulium

I'm the ugly sister of this bunch and my life is somewhat dull. While the rest of the lanthanoids are on the town, finding new jobs and teaming up in exciting technology, I tend just to sit around. Basically, I'm a bit lazy and I prefer to hide away. However, I am dragged out to be used in laser surgery and as a low-risk source of x-rays.

Date of discovery: 1879

● Density   9.321 g/cm³
● Melting point   1,545°C (2,813°F)
● Boiling point   1,950°C (3,542°F)

Tm

70 **Ytterbium**

■ The Lanthanoid Elements

* ✺ Symbol: Yb
* ✺ Atomic number: 70
* ✺ Atomic weight: 173.05
* ✺ Color: Bright silver
* ✺ Standard state: Solid at 25°C (77°F)
* ✺ Classification: Metallic

I'm your affable Swedish uncle—one of four lucky elements to be named after a small town in Sweden, called Ytterby. Many of the "rare earth" elements were discovered in minerals mined in a quarry there—this is a group that definitely like to hang out together. I am used in small quantities for lasers as well as for portable x-ray machines.

Ytterbium

Date of discovery: 1907

 Yb
* ● Density 6.57 g/cm³
* ● Melting point 824°C (1,515°F)
* ● Boiling point 1,196°C (2,185°F)

Lutetium 71

The Lanthanoid Elements

* Symbol: Lu
* Atomic number: 71
* Atomic weight: 174.97

* Color: Silver-white
* Standard state: Solid at 25°C (77°F)
* Classification: Metallic

Lutetium

I'm the last of the lanthanoid elements—soft metals with similar habits. We're bright and silvery but tarnish easily. Chemically, we tend to get up to the same tricks. I'm a French discovery, though many of my pals are Scandinavian. Dapper and well turned out, I am one of the few corrosion-resistant "rare earth" elements.

Date of discovery: 1907

* Density   9.841 g/cm³
* Melting point   1,652°C (3,006°F)
* Boiling point   3,402°C (6,156°F)

Lu

CHAPTER 11
The Actinoid Elements

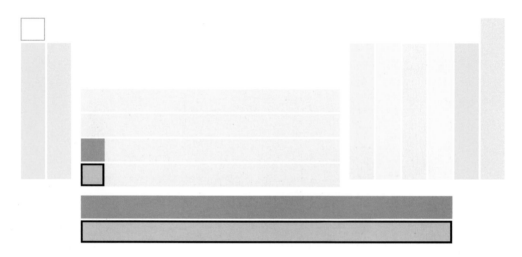

Removed from the main body of the periodic table, the actinoids are outcasts sometimes called the "f-block" elements (along with the lanthanoids). There are some seriously heavy elements here. With 89-plus protons in their nuclei, the actinoids are a bunch of dangerously radioactive misfits. Only three of them occur naturally—the rest are created artificially in nuclear reactors and particle accelerators and decay in the blink of an eye. Apart from naturally occurring uranium and thorium, these bruisers were all discovered in the 20th century.

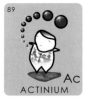
89 Ac
ACTINIUM

90 Th
THORIUM

91 Pa
PROTACTINIUM

92 U
URANIUM

93 Np
NEPTUNIUM

94 Pu
PLUTONIUM

95 Am
AMERICIUM

96 Cm
CURIUM

97 Bk
BERKELIUM

98 Cf
CALIFORNIUM

99 Es
EINSTEINIUM

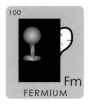
100 Fm
FERMIUM

101 Md
MENDELEVIUM

102 No
NOBELIUM

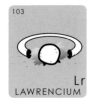
103 Lr
LAWRENCIUM

89 Actinium

■ The Actinoid Elements

- ✴ Symbol: Ac
- ✴ Atomic number: 89
- ✴ Atomic weight: 227.03
- ✴ Color: Silvery
- ✴ Standard state: Solid at 25°C (77°F)
- ✴ Classification: Metallic

I'm a ray of light—but there's nothing natural about me, sunshine. I'm entirely unearthly and shine with a spooky glow. You won't find me on the planet. I'm so radioactive —about 150 times more so than radium—that any atoms present when Earth formed have long broken down into other elements. New atoms of me are made in nuclear reactors.

Actinium

Date of discovery: 1889

 Ac :
- ● Density — 10.07 g/cm³
- ● Melting point — 1,050°C (1,922°F)
- ● Boiling point — 3,000°C (5,972°F)

Thorium 90

The Actinoid Elements

* Symbol: Th
* Atomic number: 90
* Atomic weight: 232.04

* Color: Silver-white
* Standard state: Solid at 25°C (77°F)
* Classification: Metallic

Thorium

I am "Mighty Thorium," named after the beefy Norse god Thor. I heat Earth's core. Radioactively, I'm a little tame and occur naturally. My combo with oxygen has the highest melting point of all oxides, so I'm used in the fabric-net mantles of some gas camping lamps, where I glow brightly in the flames and throw out my cheering light.

Date of discovery: 1828

* Density   11.724 g/cm³
* Melting point   1,842°C (3,348°F)
* Boiling point   4,820°C (8,708°F)

Th

91 **Protactinium**

■ The Actinoid Elements

- ✸ Symbol: Pa
- ✸ Atomic number: 91
- ✸ Atomic weight: 231.04

- ✸ Color: Bright silvery shine
- ✸ Standard state: Solid at 25°C (77°F)
- ✸ Classification: Metallic

I'm an eccentric fellow. Of no real use to anyone, I keep my activities to myself, and people leave me alone. Good news for them, I say, because my radioactivity is harmful. The atoms of most unstable, radioactive elements vanish in the blink of an eye, but some forms of me hang around almost forever. Well, I'm in no particular hurry!

Protactinium

Date of discovery: 1913

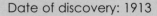

Pa :
- ● Density   15.37 g/cm³
- ● Melting point   1,568°C (2,854°F)
- ● Boiling point   4,000°C (7,232°F)

Uranium 92
The Actinoid Elements ■

- ✳ Symbol: U
- ✳ Atomic number: 92
- ✳ Atomic weight: 238.03

- ✳ Color: Gray
- ✳ Standard state: Solid at 25°C (77°F)
- ✳ Classification: Metallic

Uranium

I am a powerful force of nature. Fire a neutron at my unstable, radioactive form (atomic number 235) and my nucleus splits with a roar of energy, firing neutrons in all directions and starting a chain reaction that rips me apart! Control this reaction (called nuclear fission) and I generate power, but pack me into a bomb, and I can flatten whole cities.

Date of discovery: 1789

- ● Density   19.05 g/cm³
- ● Melting point   1,132.2°C (2,070°F)
- ● Boiling point   3,900°C (7,101°F)

U

93 Neptunium

■ The Actinoid Elements

* ✹ Symbol: Np
* ✹ Atomic number: 93
* ✹ Atomic weight: 237.05

* ✹ Color: Silvery metallic
* ✹ Standard state: Solid at 25°C (77°F)
* ✹ Classification: Metallic

As remote as the planet Neptune, I'm a mean radioactive menace. We're a nasty crew of tooled-up elements who take our gang names from the Solar System's super-cold far-off worlds—Uranus, Neptune, and Pluto. Sitting between the more famous uranium and plutonium, I am less well known and often forgotten about.

Discovered in 1940 at the University of California, Berkeley, I was the first artificially created element. I can occur naturally as a by-product of the radioactive breakdown of uranium, but this will only ever create vanishingly small amounts. I'm more commonly made as a waste product of nuclear reactors and, with a two-million-year half-life, I'm around and thoroughly nasty for a long time. I can substitute for either of my brothers in nuclear bombs, so I am a strictly controlled and heavily monitored substance.

Date of discovery: 1940

● Density   20.45 g/cm³
● Melting point 637°C (1,179°F)
● Boiling point 4,000°C (7,232°F)

Neptunium

94 **Plutonium**

■ The Actinoid Elements

- ✳ Symbol: Pu
- ✳ Atomic number: 94
- ✳ Atomic weight: 244.06

- ✳ Color: Silver-white
- ✳ Standard state: Solid at 25°C (77°F)
- ✳ Classification: Metallic

Unlike that Disney dog, life ain't no cartoon for me—I'm deadly serious. Made by nuclear scientists, a lump of me radiates heat because I release masses of radioactive alpha particles. In August 1945, a nuclear bomb made from my "239" isotope was dropped on Nagasaki in Japan. It killed or injured close to 200,000 people.

Plutonium

Date of discovery: 1940

Pu :
- ● Density   19.816 g/cm³
- ● Melting point 639.4°C (1,182.9°F)
- ● Boiling point 3,230°C (5,846°F)

Americium 95

The Actinoid Elements

- ✳ Symbol: Am
- ✳ Atomic number: 95
- ✳ Atomic weight: 243.06

- ✳ Color: Silver-white
- ✳ Standard state: Solid at 25°C (77°F)
- ✳ Classification: Metallic

Americium

I'm an all-American hero! Playing a key role in smoke alarms, I've saved countless people's lives from fire. I'm the only dangerous radioactive element allowed in your home—I had to get a special permit for it! Still, it takes less than a millionth of a gram to do the job. Sitting beneath europium on the periodic table, I'm named after America.

Date of discovery: 1789

- ● Density   12 g/cm³
- ● Melting point   1,176°C (2,149°F)
- ● Boiling point   2,607°C (4,725°F)

Am

96 Curium

The Actinoid Elements

* Symbol: Cm
* Atomic number: 96
* Atomic weight: 247.07

* Color: Silvery
* Standard state: Solid at 25°C (77°F)
* Classification: Metallic

Don't mix me up with anything health-giving—I am another no-good radioactive element. Though I wish I could "curi-um" all, I'm more likely to kill 'em! I get my name from Marie and Pierre Curie. I have had some wild, out-of-this-world times in space probes, satellites, and warming chilly robot rovers on the planet Mars.

Curium

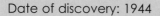

Date of discovery: 1944

 Cm:
● Density   13.51 g/cm³
● Melting point 1,340°C (2,444°F)
● Boiling point 3,110°C (5,630°F)

Berkelium 97
The Actinoid Elements ■

* Symbol: Bk
* Atomic number: 97
* Atomic weight: 247.07

* Color: Silvery
* Standard state: Solid at 25°C (77°F)
* Classification: Metallic

Berkelium

A university scientist made me in the U.S. nuclear labs at Berkeley —just like americium, californium, and a good many others. I'm a self-made whiz kid and an all-around good egg. Like all "transuranium" elements (those heavier than uranium), I'm entirely manufactured. You won't find me on Earth, and I'm gone in a flash!

Date of discovery: 1949

● Density   14.78 g/cm³
● Melting point 986°C (1,807°F)
● Boiling point   unknown

Bk

98 Californium

■ The Actinoid Elements

* Symbol: Cf
* Atomic number: 98
* Atomic weight: 251.08
* Color: Silvery
* Standard state: Solid at 25°C (77°F)
* Classification: Metallic

Born in the Golden State, I'd love to be laid-back, but the problem is my chilling ability to release streams of neutrons from my atomic nucleus. My ferocious rays can pass through an object as if it weren't there, leaving everything in its path radioactive. My neutron beams are used to kick-start nuclear reactors and to detect oil and gold.

Californium

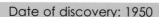

Date of discovery: 1950

Cf
● Density 15.1 g/cm³
● Melting point 900°C (1,652°F)
● Boiling point unknown

Einsteinium 99
The Actinoid Elements

* Symbol: Es
* Atomic number: 99
* Atomic weight: 252.08

* Color: Silvery
* Standard state: Solid at 25°C (77°F)
* Classification: Metallic

Einsteinium

With my crazy looks, there's no mistaking that I'm named after the famous scientist Albert Einstein. I was created in the hellish furnace of the world's first thermonuclear bomb. In 1952, the "H" bomb exploded with the energy of ten million tons of TNT, obliterating a small South Pacific island. In among the debris, sat I, beaming with radiation.

Date of discovery: 1952

* Density   13.5 g/cm³
* Melting point   860°C (1,580°F)
* Boiling point   unknown

Es

100 **Fermium**

■ The Actinoid Elements

* Symbol: Fm
* Atomic number: 100
* Atomic weight: 257.10

* Color: Unknown/silvery-gray
* Standard state: Solid at 25°C (77°F)
* Classification: Metallic

I am the periodic table's "centurion," you can always trust me to give 100 percent. I am named after the scientist who made the first nuclear reactor, Enrico Fermi. Finding a new source of power was the initial step in the U.S. project to build the terrifying weapon that brought World War II to a swift and horrific end— the atomic bomb.

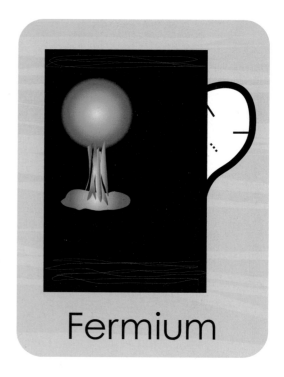

Fermium

Date of discovery: 1952

Fm

* Density — unknown
* Melting point — 1,527°C (2,781°F)
* Boiling point — unknown

Mendelevium 101
The Actinoid Elements ■

* Symbol: Md
* Atomic number: 101
* Atomic weight: 258.10

* Color: Unknown/silvery-gray
* Standard state: Solid at 25°C (77°F)
* Classification: Metallic

Mendelevium

Hooray for me, the most important element! I must be, right? After all, I'm named after that meddling Professor Mendeleev, the father of the periodic table! I'm the first "transfermium" element (heavier than fermium). Super-super-rare, I'm made in batches of a half-dozen atoms at a time and mostly I'm good for nothing!

Date of discovery: 1955

* Density   unknown
* Melting point 827°C (1,521°F)
* Boiling point   unknown

Md

102 Nobelium

■ The Actinoid Elements

- ✳ Symbol: No
- ✳ Atomic number: 102
- ✳ Atomic weight: 259.10
- ✳ Color: Unknown/metallic
- ✳ Standard state: Solid at 25°C (77°F)
- ✳ Classification: Metallic

I'm a true prizewinner! All of the dudes and dames who have had elements named after them have been great nuclear physicists making astounding discoveries... aside from me, that is. You see, I snuck in the back door, because I'm named after Alfred Nobel, who gave his name to the prize that has honored so many scientists.

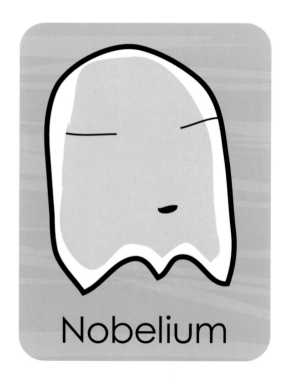

Nobelium

Date of discovery: 1966

No:
- ● Density — unknown
- ● Melting point — 827°C (1,521°F)
- ● Boiling point — unknown

Lawrencium 103
The Actinoid Elements ■

* Symbol: Lr
* Atomic number: 103
* Atomic weight: 262.11

* Color: Unknown/silvery-gray
* Standard state: Solid at 25°C (77°F)
* Classification: Metallic

Lawrencium

Pleased to meet you, please call me Lawrence. I'm the last of the actinoid elements—the long strip of superheavies at the bottom of the periodic table. I'm named after Ernest Lawrence, who built the very first "cyclotron" particle accelerators in which many of these new, unnatural elements are made.

Date of discovery: 1961

● Density   unknown
● Melting point 1,627°C (2,961°F)
● Boiling point unknown

Lr

CHAPTER 12
The Superheavies

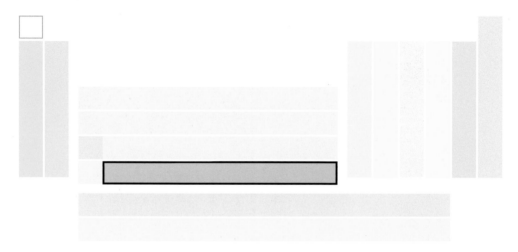

This group is totally "out there." Here at the far reaches of the periodic table live elements with atomic numbers greater than 103. These superheavy substances have all been artificially created in the lab, so most of them have only ever existed in minuscule amounts. Every single one is extremely radioactive and decays incredibly quickly. Many labs all around the world lay claim to having been the first to produce these elements, so there is always a great deal of healthy argument about what each element should be called.

104

Rf

RUTHERFORDIUM

105

Db

DUBNIUM

106

Sg

SEABORGIUM

107

Bh

BOHRIUM

108

Hs

HASSIUM

109

Mt

MEITNERIUM

110

Ds

DARMSTADTIUM

111

Rg

ROENTGENIUM

112

Cn

COPERNICIUM

104 **Rutherfordium**

■ The Superheavies

* ❋ Symbol: Rf
* ❋ Atomic number: 104
* ❋ Atomic weight: 265.12
* ❋ Color: Unknown
* ❋ Standard state: Solid at 25°C (77°F)
* ❋ Classification: Metallic

I'm the first of the "mayfly" superheavies. Entirely synthetic, we never occur in nature and don't hang around for long. Half of my atoms will have broken up within an hour. I may be quick, but it took people nearly 30 years to give me a name! After arguing about it, they settled on Ernest Rutherford, the New Zealand father of nuclear physics.

Rutherfordium

Date of discovery: 1969

Rf
* ● Density — 17 g/cm³
* ● Melting point — unknown
* ● Boiling point — unknown

Dubnium 105
The Superheavies

* Symbol: Db
* Atomic number: 105
* Atomic weight: 268.13

* Color: Unknown
* Standard state: Solid at 25°C (77°F)
* Classification: Metallic

Dubnium

Rub-a-dub-dub, I'm a champ not a chump—the longest-lived of all the superheavyweights. With an average of 28 hours before my atom decays, there's plenty of time to do some chemistry on me. This places me firmly in Group 5, with tantalum, niobium, and vanadium. My name comes from the Russian lab in which I was first discovered.

Date of discovery: 1968

● Density   21.6 g/cm³
● Melting point unknown
● Boiling point   unknown

Db

106 **Seaborgium**

■ The Superheavies

* Symbol: Sg
* Atomic number: 106
* Atomic weight: 271.13

* Color: Unknown
* Standard state: Solid at 25°C (77°F)
* Classification: Metallic

Along with the actinoid element, einsteinium, I'm the only element named after someone who was still alive at the time. . . so far! I take my sci-fi-sounding name from one Glenn T. Seaborg, who discovered ten elements in total, although *I* wasn't one of them! How weird is that? My most stable versions stick around for no more than two minutes.

Seaborgium

Date of discovery: 1974

Sg

● Density   23.2 g/cm³
● Melting point   unknown
● Boiling point   unknown

Bohrium 107
The Superheavies ▪

* Symbol: Bh
* Atomic number: 107
* Atomic weight: 270.13

* Color: Unknown
* Standard state: Solid at 25°C (77°F)
* Classification: Metallic

Bohrium

The folks who first made me wanted to call me "nielsbohrium" to honor Danish nuclear physicist Niels Bohr. In the end, they settled on boring bohrium! Just like the rest of the here-today-gone-tomorrow superheavy crew, I'm made by smashing together lighter elements in a particle accelerator. Nothing "bohrium" about that!

● Density   27.2 g/cm³
● Melting point unknown
● Boiling point   unknown

Bh

Date of discovery: 1981

108 **Hassium**

■ The Superheavies

* Symbol: Hs
* Atomic number: 108
* Atomic weight: 277.15
* Color: Unknown
* Standard state: Solid at 25°C (77°F)
* Classification: Metallic

Zip! Ping! Ten seconds and I wink out of this world. Blink and you'll miss me! It's a little bit of a hassle to make me, but that's not where I get my name. I'm named after Hesse in Germany, where I was first made in 1984. It's just one of three places in the world with the equipment to make me and and my pals. The others are Russia and the United States.

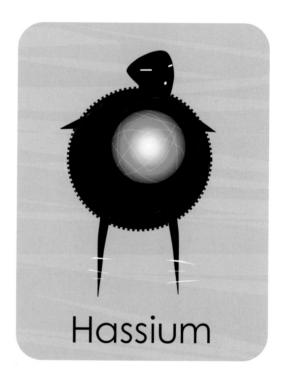

Hassium

Date of discovery: 1984

Hs
● Density   28.6 g/cm³
● Melting point unknown
● Boiling point   unknown

Meitnerium 109
The Superheavies ▪

* Symbol: Mt
* Atomic number: 109
* Atomic weight: 276.15

* Color: Unknown
* Standard state: Solid at 25°C (77°F)
* Classification: Metallic

Meitnerium

Dressed all in white and with a half-life of less than a second, no chemical experiments have ever been done with me. I was named after the German physicist Lise Meitner. She discovered nuclear fission —the process that makes nuclear bombs possible— with Otto Hahn. He got the Nobel prize, so it's only fair that Lise should get the element!

Date of discovery: 1982

● Density   28.2 g/cm³
● Melting point unknown
● Boiling point   unknown

Mt

110 **Darmstadtium**

■ The Superheavies

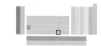

* ✹ Symbol: Ds
* ✹ Atomic number: 110
* ✹ Atomic weight: 281.16
* ✹ Color: Unknown
* ✹ Standard state: Solid at 25°C (77°F)
* ✹ Classification: Metallic

Fresh-faced and real eager to please, I'm a child of the '90s. However, since you need to make a handful of atoms of me at a time (like the rest of my superheavy brothers and sisters), and most of my atoms are gone in the blink of an eye, there's very little that you can actually *do* with me. You see, all in all, I'm something of a fusspot!

Darmstadtium

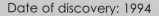

Date of discovery: 1994

Ds ● Density   27.4 g/cm³
● Melting point   unknown
● Boiling point   unknown

Roentgenium 111
The Superheavies

* Symbol: Rg
* Atomic number: 111
* Atomic weight: 280.16

* Color: Unknown
* Standard state: Solid at 25°C (77°F)
* Classification: Metallic

Roentgenium

I live life in the fast lane and love to keep the best company. I am the heaviest and newest member of the prestigious group of elements that contains copper, silver, and gold. With a half-life of around 20 seconds and only a handful of atoms of me ever having existed, I'm super-super-rare. Yep, you can call me a precious metal!

Date of discovery: 1994

* Density   24.4 g/cm³
* Melting point unknown
* Boiling point unknown

Rg

112 Copernicium

■ The Superheavies

- ✳ Symbol: Cn
- ✳ Atomic number: 112
- ✳ Atomic weight: 285.17

- ✳ Color: Unknown
- ✳ Standard state: Liquid at 25°C (77°F)
- ✳ Classification: Metallic

Artificially created in 1996, I am the last transition element. My birthplace is a famous research center in Darmstadt, Germany. I winked into existence when scientists bombarded a lead target with a beam of zinc ions.

Only about 75 atoms of my element have ever existed and, until recently, I decayed radioactively, disappearing in a millisecond. My current most stable isotope (cn-285) sticks around for 29 seconds! I hope they'll find a version of me that lasts a bit longer, so that I can be studied. There's a chance that I'm liquid at room temperature, like mercury, which would make me the second liquid metal known to science. It's enough to put your head in a whirl, which might explain why I was named after the astronomer Copernicus. He put the Sun at the center of the Solar System with the planets spinning around it.

Date of discovery: 1996

- ● Density   16.8 g/cm³
- ● Melting point   unknown
- ● Boiling point   unknown

Copernicium

INDEX

INDEX

R
radium **33**, 160
radon **138**
rare earth elements 36, 52, 140, 145, 156, 157
rhenium **67**
rhodium **58**
roentgenium **185**
rubidium **18**
ruthenium **57**
Rutherford, Ernest 178
rutherfordium **178**

S
salts 26, 32, 48, 80, 116, 122, 192
samarium **148**
scandium **36**, 52, 140
Seaborg, Glenn T. 180
seaborgium **180**
selenium **112**
silicon 24, 82, **90**, 92
silver 6, 46, 48, **60**, 84, 185
sodium **14**, 16
strontium **30**
sulfur **110**
superheavies 175, 176

T
tantalum **65**, 179
technetium **56**
terbium **151**
tellurium **113**
thallium **84**
thorium 158, **161**
thulium **155**
tin 48, 83, 86, **93**, 104
titanium **37**
transition elements 34–75, 186
transition metals 140
tungsten 64, **66**

UVW
uranium 158, **163**, 164, 169
vanadium **38**, 179

XYZ
xenon **137**
ytterbium **156**
yttrium **52**, 140
zinc 48, **50**, 85, 186
zirconium **53**

GLOSSARY

Alchemy Medieval attempts to convert base metals into gold.
Alloy A mixture of metals.
Alpha particle A positively charged particle (a helium nucleus) given off during some types of radioactive decay.
Atom The fundamental building block of all matter.
Beta particle A negatively charged particle (an electron) given off during some types of radioactive decay.
Catalyst A substance that speeds up a chemical reaction.
Compound A substance created by the chemical bonding of elements.
Electron A subatomic particle with a negative charge.
Element A substance that cannot be further broken down by chemical reactions.
Gamma ray High-energy electromagnetic radiation given off by some nuclei.
Group A vertical column of elements on the periodic table. These elements often have closely related properties.
Ion A charged particle formed when an atom loses or gains electrons.
Ionization The process of producing ions.
Isotope Atoms of the same element that have the same number of protons and electrons but differing numbers of neutrons.
Neutron A subatomic particle with a neutral charge.
Nucleus The center of an atom where protons and neutrons are found.
Oxide A compound of one element with oxygen.
Particle accelerator A machine that can produce new elements by colliding charged particles at high speeds.
Period A horizontal row of elements on the periodic table.
Proton A subatomic particle with a positive charge.
Radioactivity The spontaneous disintegration of certain nuclei accompanied by the emission of alpha, beta, or gamma radiation.
Salts Compounds formed when the hydrogen ions in an acid are replaced by metal ions or other positive ions.